Welcome...

THE GOLDEN EGG:

SUCCESSFUL BEHAVIORS, FINANCIAL SMARTS & 10 QUANTUM PRINCIPLES FOR PROSPERITY

Lateef Terrell Warnick

ISBN: 1-939199-24-7
Paperback: 978-1-939199-24-9
eBook: 978-1-939199-26-3
Library of Congress Number: 2019900610

THE GOLDEN EGG – *Successful Behaviors, Financial Smarts & 10 Quantum Principles for Prosperity*

1. Self-Help 2. Body, Mind & Spirit 3. New Age 4. Metaphysics 5. Law of Attraction 6. Warnick, Lateef Terrell I. Title

Printed in the United States of America

*"Dedicated to all the upstanding individuals who consistently strive to prosper without sacrificing their integrity or selling their soul...
This program is for you!"*

*"What lies behind us... and what lies before us...
are tiny matters compared to what lies within us!"*

Ralph Waldo Emerson

Onassis Krown LLC
"Building Kings & Queens!"
www.onassiskrown.com

Your reviews are very important to the work we do.
Our goals are to help inspire and educate the
masses on holistic living in body, mind and spirit as
well as encourage unity, love and transformation. If
you share our sentiment, then please take a
moment to leave a positive review on Amazon
and/or share on your social media outlets. Blessings!

CONTENTS

THE GOLDEN EGG:
Successful Behaviors, Financial Smarts & 10 Quantum Principles for Prosperity

INTRODUCTION:
THE GOOSE THAT LAID THE GOLDEN EGG

"A cottager and his wife had a goose that laid a golden egg every day. They supposed that the goose must contain a great lump of gold in its inside, and in order to get the gold… they killed it! Having done so, they found, to their surprise, that the goose differed in no respect from their other geese. The foolish pair, thus hoping to become rich all at once, deprived themselves of the gain of which they were assured of receiving day by day."

FOREWORD

My passion has always been to help people. As I always strive to be my best, I hope to inspire individuals to reach their greatest potential. I also believe we are three-part beings and so true transformation requires change in body mind and spirit. Therefore, all my work and service are meant to be holistic in nature. If one aspect of your being is out of balance, then your entire being will be in disharmony. What good is money without health, friends without love or work without passion? Nothing. Life without balance is an unfulfilling life.

To help others, I leverage my extensive experience in varied career fields coupled with having worked with diverse people of all backgrounds from around the world. In the military, I had the honor of serving with professionals from all walks of life. I served 10 years in the U.S. Navy and learned how to not just follow but to observe great and not-so-great leaders. I was fortunate to be able to learn from both types. I was blessed to be able to rise through the ranks quickly serving as an enlisted sailor as well as a Naval Officer to lead others. I matriculated through a great engineering curriculum in the Nuclear Power field, flight training as a student pilot and some business management skills in the Navy Supply Corp awakening my entrepreneurial spirit.

As a civilian, I enjoyed working in staffing, education, music production as well as a sales professional in telecommunications, real estate, insurance, financial services and business consultation. I've had the pleasure of consulting with entrepreneurs like contractors and photographers, small business startups in insurance and IT as well as large Fortune 100 corporations like Bank of America, Merrill Lynch, Prudential, Principal, USAA, Allstate and others. In my writings and speaking engagements, I tailor my message for the audience as well as the intention of the event. While books can be great for pointing us in the right direction, they are no substitute for personal effort and inner experience. True, eternal and everlasting prosperity isn't about money or wealth. It is always about being fulfilled and content. It is about not succumbing to fear. It is about knowing that your needs come from a Source within you and within you is the ability to overcome or transcend any situation.

I created **Onassis Krown** to help building Kings & Queens in body mind spirit as well as provide fashion, transformational coaching, inspirational travel and motivational living. I also created **1 S.O.U.L.,** an acronym for *"One Source Of Universal Love"* to assist in inspiring and uniting the masses for global transformation. I hope you enjoy this book and, most importantly, practice the techniques; for merely studying and knowing the principles are not important if you don't make the effort to change how you live.

"You must become the change you seek in the world!" **Mahatma Gandhi**

Lateef Terrell Warnick
Founder of 1 S.O.U.L. & Onassis Krown

LAYING THE FOUNDATION

The first question I'm typically asked at a book signing or presentation is, **"Why did you write this book"?** So, I figured, what better place to start than right there. As we all know, the costs of living continue to rise while our incomes seem to remain flat. While major businesses, corporations and governments try to figure how to be most effective, we as individuals must make important day-to-day decisions to "weather the storm." This book contains principles that focus on the movement of energy. The meaning of "quantum" is "any of the very small increments or parcels into which many forms of energy are subdivided." So, each principle is the breaking down of this energy associated with manifesting our intentions into smaller units that are more manageable.

We all hear a lot of fuss about education and I won't argue that education is important, not simply from the perspective that you have to have a college degree to get ahead but based in the fact that your knowledge base is your true value to yourself and to the world at large. Often, we get caught up in the dictates of society that we forget the reason why we're treading a particular path. Whether its schooling, interning or working at a job, your ability for promotion, job attainment or starting a business depends upon your knowledge base. In fact, there are only two true "talents" in life that have any value to others, and they are what we can do with our bodies in the form of sports, singing, dancing, boxing, acting etc. and the expertise knowledge we possess in our minds. To go one step further, even the best athletes, singers, dancers and actors must master the "knowledge" of their craft to become the best and truly rise above the competition.

We often hear it's *"who you know and not what you know"* and I agree that is true as far as getting your foot in the door but at the end of the day if you're not qualified for the job then it doesn't matter if the president of the company is your father. He won't be in business for long if he puts people in positions they're not equipped to handle or can perform efficiently within. So, who you may know is certainly helpful in networking and getting the opportunity for consideration, but it definitely will not "close the deal" for you. **What you know** is of true value!

Second to your knowledge base, and depending upon the circumstances, your people skills are next in the line of importance for breeding success. If two candidates are equally qualified for a job, promotion or opportunity then the person with the better ability to relate to the decision-maker, and ultimately the audience he or she will be serving, will typically gain the favor. Go to any government held office or company position and you will find extremely smart people that are not where they "should be" because they haven't developed the effective communication and people-skills necessary. A lot of people falsely believe that they were just born with a certain personality and cannot change. This is not true! A lot of successful comedians and performers were introverts as children and still prefer to "keep to themselves" as adults. However, they nurtured their

6

craft to be able to "step outside of themselves" and shine in front of audiences when expressing their talent.   With the appropriate time, focus and determination, you can create the necessary "persona" to succeed in the work place or any arena. Muhammad Ali, the former world champion boxer and civil rights figure is a perfect example of this fact.

Now truth be told, a person's knowledge base and people skills may tend to be the most obvious and examinable traits they possess but if two individuals are comparable in these areas, what causes one to have surpassed another?   The differences tend to be of a much subtler nature and yet are the most profound in determining a person's experience in life.   It is a result of that person's internal dialogue.   Our perception, our thought patterns and what we tell ourselves greatly influence our experiences. Likewise, what things happen to us in our daily lives is interpreted by our minds therefore telling us what our "reality" is and hence influences our actions and thus the cycle repeats itself – observation, perception, thoughts, emotions, actions, experience, reaction and back to observation. This is pretty much the process of our interaction with the world around us.

Of course, this is extremely difficult to witness and examine because we can't monitor a person's actions completely in a 24-hour day nor can we look inside their heads. However, through case studies, surveys, experiments, psychology, science, medicine and metaphysics we begin to see patterns emerge that show commonalities of people of various groups. In fact, through quantum physics we are beginning to see more and more evidence that conclude one's experience is a direct result of their thoughts and choices. These studies have evolved into the phenomenon known as the "Laws of Attraction."

Many, however, don't know the history of how the concept of the Laws of Attraction came about and unfortunately a lot of authors on this subject don't do a very good job of explaining or tracing these facts. The most obvious ancestors of this "philosophy" would be mystic thought and metaphysics popularized by the Egyptians, Greeks and various renaissance and enlightenment periods in Europe and the Americas. Many eastern teachings such as Buddhism likewise focus on the connection between the mind and body. If you study the Bible from an esoteric approach, the quotes of Jesus also seem to resonate these truths.

Through my research, I must accredit most of these concepts to Sanatana Dharma, which means "Eternal Law." Most modern thought equates Sanatana Dharma with Hinduism, but this is still quite a misnomer. The term Hindu began by foreign outsiders coming to the Asian continent to identify the natives in the area of the Sindhu River. Hinduism is based upon various Holy Scriptures mainly the Vedas and Upanishads amongst some other prominent writings. However, the word Hindu is never found in these texts and Sanatana Dharma is said to precede even the Vedas, which most accept to be the oldest scriptures in the world. Legend has it that when God or Spirit manifests creation, He/She/It establishes this "Eternal Law" so that mankind will always be able to retrace its footsteps back towards its true spiritual essence.

The great thing about these "laws" is that you don't necessarily have to be religious or believe in God in order to incorporate, apply and take advantage of the knowledge. Like a scientist, you are free to experiment with the tools made available to see if they hold any truth for you. Similarly, a person never has to enter a laboratory or see an atom to take advantage of the fact that when you turn on the light switch, electricity empowers lighting and other appliances for your benefit.

For those who are already familiar with the concepts of the Laws of Attraction, many have been left "hanging" without some sort of practical program or approach to implement into their daily lives. Some followers of the Laws of Attraction have tried for years to alter their thinking and speech in hopes of changing their experiences. Yet there are many successful people in this world who have never made any effort to incorporate Laws of Attraction, however, they continue to enjoy all the benefits that money can allow. So, what is the difference that allows a person who is totally ignorant of the Laws of Attraction to prosper and yet someone who struggles to implement these laws day after day but still can't seem to succeed?

Well, the first thing we must acknowledge, which unfortunately a lot of Law of Attraction books fail to address, is that we are three-part beings of body, mind and soul. Again, if you're the non-religious type who may not believe in a God or even a soul, then simply think of your soul as the consciousness that makes you... you! When you strip away all the things of your life that you identify with and silence the body and mind there will still be the essence of you that knows "I exist!" Most of us live day-to-day allowing the body's experiences to dictate to the mind and consequentially the soul consciousness. In fact, the reverse should be true and **is** true. The soul consciousness precedes all! The soul is the precursor to the mind and the mind **should** have dominion over the body although this is not always the case. Many of us have become slaves to the demands of the body.

Most Law of Attraction books would have you believe that all you must do is "think happy thoughts" and all will be well! While in an absolute sense they may be correct, there are some huge disclaimers that must be stated. Again, not to get too deep in to scriptures but if you believe that there have been persons who have walked this earth able to perform miracles and defy the laws of nature, it is because they became to embody the understanding between the connection of soul, mind and body. Let me be very clear – the vast majority of the people reading this book are no where near the stage of being able to materialize precise experiences directly as a result of their "thought power."

I think that deserves reiteration. Do not think by simply reading this book or any other book on the Law of Attraction that all you have to do now is sit back and think your way to millions of dollars! You must first come to understand and respect the Laws of Nature before you can learn to "bend them." To paint an analogy, do you think simply from reading a health magazine full of body builders that you can now go into a gym and bench press a 500-pound dead weight? I hope not because chances are you will get your chest caved in! It takes time and consistent practice to advance to that ability to lift that sort of weight. Likewise, it takes significant practice and technique to wield the ability to manifest your desires through sheer thought and will.

So, this leads to the reason as to why I decided to write this book. From what I've seen in the marketplace and from the many lectures, seminars and videos I've witnessed, the majority of these "Law of Attraction" teachings are doing the reader a disservice by leading them to believe that all you must do is counter every "negative" experience with a happy thought and the battle is won. No, you must be practical in your approach and strengthen your ability to "evolve" your current state of awareness through regular practice and a regiment.   I feel my history and experiences have uniquely qualified me to bring together key ingredients necessary to implement a strategy to help you bring about a greater experience of prosperity in your life.

This is where most "Law of Attraction" authors or salesmen rather give you their resume to show you how you too can make millions of dollars by simply buying their product and following their recipe which they typically define as "effortless." I've worked in sales for many years and we learned many psychological tactics to get people to buy a product. It may vary in order or technique but essentially boils down to this. People are driven by fear and greed! This is what drives the entire financial markets. When things are going well, people like to buy which normally means they're buying high. When attitudes are negative then people start selling in order to "protect" what they still have and this merely precipitates more fear, which then drives markets down compounding the effect.

Well, the sales process essentially works the same way. The salesman knows when a customer is first approached their tension levels are high and they're on defense. So, the salesman tries to gain your trust by small talk, building rapport and finding something in common with you. Once you're able to let your guard down a little bit they then get you to open up by sharing simple facts about themselves with the intent of you doing the same in response. We as human beings by nature tend to be reciprocal. If someone does us a favor or shares something private, we feel a sense of duty or "obligation" to return the same. Once they get you talking then the goal is to find out what your "hot buttons" are such as your life goals, dreams, ambitions and what's most important to you.

Once they get you "visualizing" they then try to reintroduce that tension and fear you had at the beginning of your meeting but now since they've 'befriended" you they act as if they are on your side. There are different ways to get people to buy or take action, but in the world we live in, FEAR always seems to be the most effective. People tend to buy off of emotion, so they need to hit those emotional triggers to get you to *"sign on the dotted line"* with your cash or credit card. They convince you that if you don't have their product, solution or service then you're vulnerable and that fear will consume your happiness or lifestyle. These salesmen try to make you feel special, smarter than others or unique by reconfirming you on your decision to "buy now!" Additionally, they convince you it is an urgent matter to take action now otherwise their product might not be available tomorrow. The truth is most of these salesmen who use these tactics made their riches not from their own product but by convincing you to buy their product. In other words, they don't let you in on their **real** secret. I equate them to the people, I'm sure you've seen before, who tell you how you're going to get wealthy from their real estate secrets. Apparently, they've made so much money that they're simply tired of it and now they just want to show others how to make more money than they can handle. If they're tired of making so much money, couldn't they just tell you how to do it rather than make you pay to find out?

But you can see right through their little schemes if you just use a little common sense. Most of these salesmen have their own companies and employees. Now ask yourself, "Why would this person possibly have employees if their **'secret'** was so sure-proof?!" Wouldn't all of their employees who were in on the secret just go out and make ten times more money by implementing the strategies and starting their own companies? Wouldn't that employee prefer to make more money, call his or her own shots and write someone else a paycheck rather than have to wait for one? Some old adages are true, ***"If it sounds too good to be true... it probably is too good to be true!"*** I've worked in various business capacities, finances and investments for a long time and I have yet to come across a "guaranteed" opportunity that is sure to make you rich.

So, since my approach to prosperity isn't so much about money, I will "qualify" myself differently without bragging about how much money I make or how listening to me is going to make you wealthy.

Let me say this, prosperity isn't about discovering some "secret." It is, however, about discovering yourself! What I mean by this is most of us from birth have been conditioned to think, speak and behave in certain ways molded by our parents, peers and society as a whole. Many of us have never really taken the time to separate ourselves from the outer noise, look within and see what makes us unique. What makes me tick? Prosperity begins with knowing yourself, confidently expressing yourself and having the courage to do what you love while impacting those around you in a positive way. When you are able to do these things effectively, all that you need will manifest for you to enjoy life to the fullest.

So, to tell you about what I've been able to accomplish myself, let me share a few tidbits. I started a Social Network that focuses on subject matter most important to me. I attract others who are in harmony with its ideals. I started my own publishing company and release my own books. I also founded a non-profit organization, which again attempts to make changes that are important to me. Simply by using these three avenues, I am able to make a comfortable living doing what I enjoy most and helping others in the process. I also invest in other companies and businesses through the stock market as well as personal relationships of business owners I know who provide services in such a way that makes their communities better. Let me share a few numbers just to put things in perspective.

Obviously, from running a non-profit you get to receive donations from others, and you get the tax benefits of write offs. By law, however, you have the right to not only pay a staff but yourself as well a "reasonable" compensation in performing the mission of the organization. Secondly, by controlling a social network, I have the control to attract advertisers who then pay me for exposure to members of my site. As the network grows and attracts more members, I can theoretically charge comparable fees that advertisers will pay for the potential new business. As far as my books go, since I control all the rights, I make a much larger profit margin than many best-selling authors who have publishing deals with major houses. These authors may typically make $1-$1.50 per book sale. So, to make a hundred thousand dollars they must sell somewhere between 66,666 to 100,000 units. Depending on the type of book sale, I stand to make on the low end $4 to as much as $10 per book. Other products generate greater profits but to make $100,000 I only need to sell between 10,000 to 25,000 units. So, for achieving only 10-25% of a best-seller's success, I make just as much money, have more creative control and can change my prices whenever I choose. Most importantly, I don't have to "sell my soul" using aggressive sales tactics or swindling people out of their money. I can look any supporter or reader of my works in the face and maintain my integrity. This is a fundamental part of being happy and feeling prosperous! You don't have to be a millionaire to have plenty of freedom to do all the things you enjoy because your attitude is already one of contentment. In fact, it is precisely this attitude that will in time draw those "millions" to you when you least expect it and are not even looking for it.

     "Fortune is like a flirt; she cares not for him who wants her, but she is at the feet of him who does

not care for her. Money comes and showers itself upon one who does not care for it; so does fame come in abundance until it is a trouble and a burden. They always come to the Master. The slave never gets anything. The Master is he who can live in spite of them, whose life does not depend upon the little, foolish things of the world." Swami Vivekananda

As stated previously, as three-part beings of body, mind and soul we must (for the time being) act as such and ensure our consciousness, thoughts and actions all coincide to produce prosperity. As a former Naval Officer, I had ten years of experience first as an enlisted member taking orders and implementing the "game plan" and also as a junior officer responsible for delegating theses plans to the ranks that were going to help accomplish the mission. Of course, the military is well known for its training, organization, discipline, planning, coordinating, coaching and structure. The military does a good job of defining the mission and communicating what the desired end result will be.

I've also worked as a Licensed Financial Advisor for several Fortune 100 companies. My job was to work with average every day working families as well as high net worth individuals investing millions of dollars, planning for retirement, saving for children's education, starting and growing businesses, budgeting and making large purchases and protecting their assets from accidents, unexpected events or death. Obviously, this isn't a physically demanding job but certainly can be very mentally taxing and requires great attention to detail.

Lastly, I've been a metaphysician and yogi since the early years of my life. I've learned from and studied the teachings of various saints, sages, yogis and spiritual adepts. From my extensive research on these teachings from around the globe and from all cultures, I've come to recognize the common truths and to convey, what are sometimes rather intricate concepts, into layman terms. These teachings are accepted as a "science" because many adepts throughout the centuries have tested them and proven the same results each and every time. You too can do the same as long as you have the willingness, patience and determination to incorporate the techniques.

So, to try and make this reading a little fun, I've adopted three "personas" to bring together a more concise and clear approach to hopefully produce the greatest results. I will share what I've listed as ten quantum principles essential to creating prosperity. To address what one needs to do with their body for success, I've enlisted the services of the *"Coach."* To address the mental needs from a financial perspective I'll do so as the *"Advisor."* To address the involvement of the consciousness or soul, I'll speak as the *"Yogi."* I believe all things begin with spirit, but I may change the order of presentation throughout the chapters depending on which I feel may have the greatest significance to that principle. In the end you should have gained some knowledge and insight on what area(s) you may be lacking that you need to strengthen in order to change your experience.

Before we jump into the ten principles, I would like to address one last thing that may seem minor but is indeed significant and that is the title of this book.   Each word and phrase were carefully selected to convey the most appropriate idea. First, I created an acronym for the word **P.R.O.S.P.E.R.I.T.Y.** and redefine it as the:

"Principle Reasons Optimistic Service Produces Exponential Richness Inevitably Through You!"

Prosperity begins with "giving" something of value to another person. It doesn't mean giving money to every homeless person on the street unless that's what you enjoy doing. What it does mean is to give in the capacity that you are able. Give love, patience, understanding, guidance, knowledge, wisdom, peace, blessings, prayers, laughter, joy, bliss, happiness, assistance, help, a shoulder to cry on or so forth... Become a giver and you open up the floodgates of blessings to return to you. If you don't want to call them blessings, then simply accept the type of energy you put out will return to you in like kind. Remember, the person you give to may not be in a position to give back, but you shouldn't worry about that. Nothing you give ever goes in vain. What you put out comes back to you. What goes around comes around. The more unselfishly, thoughtfully, sincerely and optimistically you are able to give, the greater your energy multiplies and flies back to you!

The point is we must begin to redefine what prosperity means. Many of us always think that being prosperous is a degree of what we accumulate. This is very limited thinking which is self serving and even if you were to amass wealth, chances are you wouldn't get the fulfillment you had hoped for nor would it last. Regardless of how long you live, you will have to part with your riches upon death. The essence of being prosperous is to be happy, fulfilled and content in body, mind and spirit. It doesn't require a stretch of the imagination to recognize that having millions of dollars isn't very satisfying if I have to exchange my physical health for it. I assure you any handicapped person would happily trade in all of their money to be able to use their full body again. Likewise, what good is a strong and beautiful body if our minds are haunted with paranoia, depression and stress? So, if you're reading this book with the intention of simply figuring out how to become the next billionaire then this isn't the right book for you. If on the other hand, your idea of prosperity coincides with mine, which is to be healthy in body, mind & spirit, live comfortably doing what you love surrounded by good people who share in your prosperity then I invite you to continue along!

Lastly, I could have called this the 10 "Laws of Attraction" or the 10 "Rules" etc but to me when most people use the word **law** they do so in the context of physics or mathematics to suggest if *"a + b = c therefore c − b = a"* However, when it comes to subtle things such as our thoughts, that generate creative energy, it is almost impossible to take a group of people and have them all create the same result. For example, I could give your very precise instructions to perform an act a certain way and you still may not get the same outcome as myself. If I push on the wall with ten Newtons of force and you push on the same wall with ten Newtons of force, observation may tell us that we both performed the same act identically but in actuality everything from the size of our hands, bodies, the thoughts in our heads, our emotions, all the way down to our very atoms will have produced different experiences for us. Our experiences are as unique as our fingerprints. I will expand on this more towards the end of the book. I also chose to not call these "rules" because they tend to convey the limiting idea that you **must** do something. We all, obviously, have the freedom to do as we choose. The real question is, are we happy with what our actions are producing for us?

I purposefully chose to use the word **principle** in the sense of meaning: "an underlying factor or endowment" in a concept or practice. Until you are able to master these concepts, you should think of them as principles rather than laws. Another distinction is that I believe we are **Creators** and not **Attractors**. God doesn't attract anything; He merely creates. Similarly, we are creators and our lives are a reflection of our thoughts and thus we're technically not attracting anything either. Everything we experience is a result of what we create either consciously or subconsciously. Our experiences aren't truthfully attracted to us rather they are a result of us. I will attempt to go into further detail on these concepts when explaining the principles.

When I joined the Navy, I was enlisted as a nuclear machinist mate. For approximately two years we studied all sorts of mathematics, calculus, physics, chemistry, electricity and so forth. At various points in time, we would come across a topic that would provoke many questions from the students. The Instructors would do their best to explain the answers but in truth certain concepts weren't fully understood. There are a lot of "laws" in science that are honestly just theories. The fact of the matter is some things are so difficult to observe through experimentation that scientists have no choice but to conclude that this must be the way it works. In other words, we may at times have to use deductive reasoning to work backwards that this is the result and we "believe" that this is why it happens this way.

For example, we can't really see electrons, but we know through experimentation that they carry certain charges and operate in certain ways and thus conclude they exist. Until another scientist comes along and "proves" that they don't exist, we have to accept it as truth since all indicators suggest that in deed they must exist. So, whenever we would reach one of these crossroads that science has yet to fully unravel, the instructors would tell us to simply hit the *"I believe"* button so we can move on. Likewise, we can debate certain topics through numerous journals and still not be able to "prove" things work a certain way. Since this isn't intended to be a science journal, I'll do my best to explain certain concepts but at some point in time, if your intellectual thirst still isn't satisfied, then you'll simply have to hit the "I believe" button (at least for the time being) and move on so that you can attempt to apply and/or experiment with the principles to see if they produce results for you.

I've attempted to list these 10 principles in their most logical order. The more skilled you become in one principle, the transition to the next should come all that more easily. In fact, the progression should not only make sense but also allow you to smoothly master the techniques. Some principles may prove to be a little more challenging than others, but your approach should be a balance between effort and non-effort. Don't get overly caught up in evaluating yourself and understand that changes tend to be subtle and happen gradually. Your age has no direct bearing upon your success at incorporating these principles, however, realize that depending on your current perspective, thoughts and ways you process information, it will take some time to make changes in your psyche. Self-introspection can be a challenging task if you're not used to attempting it but with due time and practice it'll become second nature to you. This book may also prove to be one you may have to revisit from time to time as you gain more experience and insight from life. Learning should be a life long process. You're never too old to change or learn new tricks. We are "diamonds in the rough" in the process of being continuously refined to at last we become sparkling diamonds! Some changes won't be recognizable until hindsight affords you the opportunity to examine it from another perspective. Be patient and consistent and you'll master all of these principles in time.

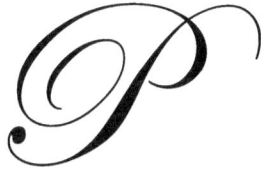

THE PRINCIPLE OF PRESENCE

"The golden opportunity you are seeking is in yourself. It is not in your environment; it is not in luck or chance, or the help of others; it is in yourself alone."

Orison Swett Marden

Yogi says...

Everything begins with presence! Eckhart Tolle, yogis, coaches and trainers along with many athletes, artists and everyone who seeks to perform at their highest-level attest that being present is essential. Presence means not being scattered or distracted. Presence is being aware, conscious and focused; presence goes hand in hand with execution. So, what exactly is presence? Presence is power! Presence is our ability to be still in body, mind and spirit. When we are able to filter out all the outer distractions that come in the form of noises, stimuli, restless thoughts and so forth and just try to be alone for a moment, we become more present in the moment of now. As I stated, we as souls are essentially pure consciousness.

The soul has no gender, race, age or nationality. The soul is not a parent nor a child nor a sibling nor has any obligations or responsibilities or burdens. The soul just simply is! The soul is equally as difficult, if not impossible, to define as God may be; hence, why we are made in our Creator's image. God needs nothing, asks for nothing nor seeks anything. He is sufficient unto Himself. Our souls likewise demand of nothing nor need anything to exist. It is because we identify with our bodies that we feel like we need things. Spirit and the soul exist in spite of and beyond all created matter. The soul is intangible and formless and doesn't take up any space. It is best to just think of it as your consciousness, your sense of being. If I asked you to show me where your consciousness is, you wouldn't be able to do so. We may feel our consciousness is in our brains but that is simply because most thought processes and creative energy is concentrated there but they are an expression of our consciousness and not the cause of our consciousness. This may be a difficult concept for some to grasp so you may just have to hit the "I believe" button but rest assured this is the case.

To go one step further, everything that takes up space or consists of matter is therefore temporary and transient. If it has a beginning, then it must have an end. Spirit and the soul do not require space and therefore are the only true or ultimate "realities." Spirit is permanent because It is unmanifested. Yet It is the Cause of all things manifest. Time as we know it is really the observed result of the change between two relative objects. Spirit is Absolute and has no relative object to quantify It. Time does not exist for Spirit and because the soul, being

26

"individualized spirit," likewise is not subject to time and therefore has no beginning or end. Quantum Physics is beginning to see these correlations. Einstein went to his grave trying to prove a "theory of everything." In essence all matter mysteriously comes from nowhere. We may call it space or ether but literally all matter "pops" up from nothingness. Hence, all matter will equally "dissolve" back into this nothingness. The reason is because all matter begins merely as an idea.

All ideas possess creative energy. This creative energy behaves as "waves" of intelligence vibrating with life. Through science, we observe these waves as photons, quarks, electrons and ultimately atoms, which are the building blocks of all creation. But all matter begins simply as an idea and continues to exist, for however long, only as long as we choose and will for it to do so. Thus all tangible things are a result of two main ingredients – choice and will!   As choosers, we simply desire to experience various relative "things" from an infinite basket of possibilities. Man truly is not capable of thinking of an original idea since all ideas stem from this Original Infinite Source of Possibilities – God. Again, this isn't meant to be a theology discussion so if you believe in the "big bang" then God would be that Source that existed or gave rise to matter prior to the big bang.

All matter is subject to the laws of physics and yet it is apparent that there is/was an Intelligent Force that caused matter to become planets, stars, and galaxies and gave rise to intelligent life, as we know it. We as individuals merely select or "scoop" cupfuls of this infinite ocean of ideas and energy. We may not recognize that this is what we are doing but this in essence is how it works. The degree to which we are able to manifest ideas and hence create experiences varies to the degree of our will and the "size of our cups."

Those people with the greater degree of clarity, vision and will are able to manifest the objects of their choosing more efficiently and solidly. So if you want to be able to create greater prosperity, happiness, health, love or otherwise, you must increase your clarity of thought, the energy of your vision and your strength of will. How do we achieve these necessary qualities? We do so by practicing greater Presence. Think of your body, mind, life and experiences as a rechargeable battery. If you constantly use your battery to power the lights, the radio, the television and so forth then you drain the battery more quickly and it dies. In order to utilize it again you must recharge it. Our bodies and minds likewise are always occupied with various tasks required of us throughout the day. The more we do, the more quickly we become drained and typically require sleep to recharge.

Sleep for most of us is the only way that we "reconnect" to the actual Power Source, which is Spirit. Sleep, however, isn't always the most efficient way to recharge although it may be the only way we know how. It is unfortunate that many people don't even get restful sleep so they go through their day already feeling drained so they just have to cope. Sleep does recharge our bodies fairly effectively for those who do get rest but it primarily affects our minds subconsciously. We do gain some mental peace but this can often be short-lived depending on how our day goes. To top this off, most of us don't breath properly as well which makes our bodily systems work harder and less efficiently thereby making us more fatigued.

So what Presence does for us is to try and consciously recharge ourselves to gain the greatest benefit. As beginners, we may not initially feel the impact but to simply find some time within your day either morning, lunchtime or evening to isolate yourself from all outer disturbances will do wonders for you. Try to find a quiet place, assume a comfortable sitting position, slow down your breathing, erect your spine, inhale deeply, hold for a few seconds and then exhale fully. By relaxing your body and calming your respiration you'll directly calm your mind as well. When we are able to significantly calm our bodies and minds then the **little light** of our souls begins to flicker! The soul is able to connect to the still Spirit within and in essence becomes "recharged" with vital energy. This vital energy comes from an Infinite Source, being Spirit, and manifests itself in all capacities of intelligence, vitality, creativity, intuition and any variation needed for us to live prosperously. I encourage you to either obtain some literature on meditation, find a yoga class or simply follow the basic techniques of sitting still, relaxing the body, calming the breath and thoughts. Start with a few minutes that you are able to maintain but with continued practice you'll be able to remain in this relaxed state longer and receive the essential benefits. This is the first and most crucial stage to strengthening your will power and magnifying the "size of your cup."

Spiritual Practice: *Establish a routine effective immediately to be alone and focus your attention within to develop greater presence.*

Advisor says...

So what does being present mean mentally, related to understanding money? Being present when it comes to financial smarts stems from educating yourself and always being aware of where you stand financially speaking. In other words, you should be able to rattle off the top of your head a fairly accurate assessment of what your net worth is, what your monthly income is and what your monthly outflow may be. I assure you the vast majority of people have no clue what these numbers are which means they're not taking the most effective approach towards managing their money. I understand that these figures may vary somewhat from month to month but this shouldn't be drastic unless something unexpected happens.

Some people say "money is the root of all evil" but let's be honest you cannot survive in this world without it. So until the entire world economy somehow changes, we must play the game to the best of our abilities so that we not only stay afloat but hopefully experience smooth sailing. The way to achieve this reality is to begin to take ownership of your finances. You don't have to be a math wizard to know if I spend more than I make that I will ultimately end up deeply in a hole that I may not be able to get myself out.

Most educated people are aware that not only have the costs of living gone up but the increases in salaries have not comparatively, yet there are people who become wealthy every single day. Everyone is not going to become an accountant or investment advisor so if numbers aren't your forte then you need to acquire the services of someone who can manage them for you. However, never, ever depend on that person to totally manage your money as if it were his or her own. If you made the money then you need to assume the responsibility that it is in your vital interest to maintain it. You have to know what level of risk your are comfortable with, you must continually review how its being managed, not to the point of being obsessed, but enough to know that you're comfortable with the day to day fluctuations.

This starts with the basics. Whatever your income may be, you should always pay yourself first! Decide how much you can comfortably put aside each pay period. Many suggest 10% or more but you have to decide what position you're in to save. Now there are several ways to "pay yourself." The first is to simply have an emergency savings fund. A comfortable emergency savings will typically be around 3 to 6 months worth of whatever your monthly living expenses are. So if all your monthly living expenses add up to... let's just say... $3000 then you should try to keep anywhere from $9000 to $12000 in a safe keeping.

Now by safekeeping I'm not suggesting in your backyard or between your mattresses. Your money should always be making money even if it's just a very small percentage. Most savings accounts are federally insured up to a certain amount. This may vary on how the accounts are set up, how many banks you have it spread across, your marriage status and whose name(s) you have the accounts listed under. I'll shy away from specifics since everyone's situation is unique and you need to speak to a professional who can look at your assets and your particular needs to give you the best advice on where to place your money.

I personally don't keep too much money in regular savings accounts since the returns tend to be miniscule. I prefer money market accounts. These tend to be very safe places to keep your money and will typically give you better returns. Of course you want to bear in mind that bank products such as a savings account will have the FDIC insurance to protect you in case your bank fails while most money markets won't although some do. Again you must know the particulars of what your financial institution has to offer.

Along with these basics, you must also be aware of your credit status at all times. I recommend using a credit reporting service. These services have substantially come down in prices over the years and chances are your bank offers this service. I think it is well worth the money to know if someone fraudulently attempts to apply for something in your name, if the car company you shopped with to buy a vehicle is still pulling your credit years after the purchase or if the parking ticket you got while out of town and forgot to pay has now been sent to collections and is showing on your credit report. Your credit report is like your school grades. You may have straight A's but get that one F and suddenly your GPA drops drastically. **Never late** is better... but **late is still better than never!** The sooner you're able to challenge negative items on your credit report, the better your score will be and the less impact it'll have on you.

The next basic yet important tactic to use in managing your dollars is to start planning for retirement as early as you begin working! As I already stated, the costs of living continue to climb while incomes don't and unless you want to work till you die, it behooves you to start as early in your life as possible. Not only do you get tax breaks from the government but also, depending on your employer, you may get free money towards your 401k or whatever retirement vehicle they may offer. If your company doesn't have any retirement plans then any working person should be eligible for an IRA. Again, you want to talk to an advisor to look at your situation to recommend the best account for you to use. Some people reading this may be in the latter part of their working careers and may not have a retirement plan. Do not use this as an excuse. It doesn't matter how old you are, start something now! Some growth is better than none and if you make smart decisions, you never know how your fortune may turn for the better so establish the right behaviors now and we'll worry about some of those other bridges when we get to them.

Now one quick thing about your Financial Advisor, it helps to know how he or she gets paid. Many advisors work off of commission so there's an incentive for them to sell certain products. Depending on the product, they may have to disclose what that is by law but this is not always the case. So based upon the character of your advisor they may at times be in a direct conflict between your best interests and their own. Who do you think is typically going to win in that battle? If you think it's you then I got some ocean front property I'd like to sell you in Kansas. No, silly, your advisor more times than not is going to do what puts the biggest commission in their pockets. Not always because they're just trifling but because they have employers who put pressure on them to sell certain products. The profit motive can be one of the most corruptible traits of any business. Hence, part of the reason we experienced the whole recent financial meltdown. Many banks and investment firms were gambling with people's money in investments that had no true value and this gamble was passed along in the form of incentives all the way from the top, to the advisors, loan departments, realtors and anyone who stood to make a profit.

I'll stop preaching for now but it always behooves you to have the presence of mind to know where you stand financially. As your life and circumstances change so should your money management requirements. If an advisor is giving you advice that doesn't feel right or doesn't sit right with you then like any doctor's assessment, you should get a second opinion. There are advisors who work off of fees or even just a base salary. I'm not suggesting that they still don't have their own incentives that may cloud their advice but getting advice from perhaps 2 or 3 different advisors who all get paid differently may help you to find the "middle path" that is most comfortable and conducive to your overall financial well being.

Financial Tip: *Take charge of your finances now by educating yourself and steering your financial health in the direction you choose.*

Coach says...

Having presence of body starts with good health. Since this isn't a health and fitness discussion I won't go into details on a exercise regiment rather I want to stress the importance of physical health towards the attainment of a prosperous life. As I stated earlier, to truly be prosperous we must be so in body, mind and spirit. The state of our physical body directly influences our state of mind and vice versa. So to truly be whole and get the most out of life, we must have healthy bodies to enjoy it. If you're not already doing so I encourage you to try to incorporate some sort of physical exercise into your daily routine or at least 4-5 times per week.

Not only will you look better and be happier with your body but additionally your physical appearance will influence you emotionally for the better as well as improve your self-confidence and esteem in interacting with the world. Beyond this, your efforts to strengthen your health also help to strengthen your will power. Most people don't enjoy the act of exercising unless you're one of those "weird" people that get enjoyment from pain. ☺ But seriously, although in the midst of exercise we may struggle, we do typically feel improvements in our vitality, strengthened immune systems and less frequent colds or sicknesses and better sleep at night as well with continued effort. More importantly, a strong body will help you to gain greater presence of mind and spirit, which opens you up to the infinite potentiality within you.

I personally try to start each workday in the morning with 30 minutes to an hour of exercise. Afterwards, I take a shower, which relaxes my muscles and my mind as well as opens up the pores. From there I try to spend at least an hour in yoga practice and meditation. This is my routine for establishing that presence in body, mind and spirit. It requires some discipline and some days seem to be a little more auspicious than others but the more you commit to a routine, the more effective and natural it will ultimately become for you.

Now what does all this being **present** do for you? It allows you to think more clearly, focus on your goals, become more organized, remain calmer in various situations throughout the day and make you more efficient in your time management. Another aspect of being present in body is to establish the necessary discipline to always know what you should be doing at any given time of the day. I encourage people to be very detailed oriented when it comes to managing your time, almost to the point of being anal. My process is to essentially program everyday into my smart phone down to the minute of when I check emails, when I read or write, when I make important phone calls, when I take breaks, when I take lunch, when I run errands and so forth. Obviously, unexpected items often come up or I may stray from the road but the point is the more days you're able to adhere to a routine, the more productive you'll be and the more results you'll make towards your goals.

No one will be 100% on target in their day to day dealings but as long as you're close or in the 90 percentile, then you'll be much further along than if you continuously just "wing it" everyday. Having a fairly strict routine will help to keep you more accountable. Don't become so rigid to the point that you're stressing or punishing yourself for "goofing off" because you got an unexpected visit or phone call from a friend. Remember part of prosperity is enjoying life. At the end of your days when your life flashes in front of you, the sincere moments of laughter and fun you shared with friends and family will stand out and be the most memorable. Be organized and disciplined but remember to have fun and be present in the moment to truly enjoy it all.

Success Skill: *Do whatever it takes to nurture good health. If you lack the willpower find a workout buddy or personal trainer to help you. As the years pass, you'll be grateful you did!*

*"As we let our light shine, we unconsciously give other people permission to do the same. As we are liberated from our own fear, our **presence** actually liberates others."*

Marianne Williamson

THE PRINCIPLE OF CREATIVITY

"Creative activity could be described as a type of learning process where teacher and pupil are located in the same individual."

Arthur Koestler

Yogi says...

As you continue to practice presence, you'll inevitably begin to strengthen your intuition and receive creative ideas that seem to come from nowhere. This can be a blessing and can likewise feel like a curse at times. It depends on perspective and what your goals may be. Practicing presence is typically the means and the goal in itself. In other words, the calmness, peace and serenity in body and mind are sufficient reward enough. However, creative ideas tend to be a byproduct of practicing stillness. My suggestion is that you set a time that you intend to practice silence and try not to allow anything to interrupt that time. Start with something that is comfortable for you and with practice gradually increase the length of time. For a beginner, 15 minutes may seem like an eternity but try to set that as a goal. In time, you'll be able to increase it to 30, 45 and 60 minutes. You can choose to call this meditation, yoga or simply being alone, ideally without thoughts, but in the beginning they will certain be there with you.

Like I said, your thoughts will be difficult to suppress so there's no need to worry about ideas coming to you. Most of the thoughts that enter your mind will be like static coming from a radio that isn't properly tuned. These are essentially just junk thoughts that may be on your mind like lunch, bills, errands you're supposed to run, something a boss or coworker may have said to you etc. But as you are able to maintain some inner calmness, it'll be like tuning in and hitting that right frequency of your favorite music station.

You'll have a thought or two that seems to stand out from the rest. It may be you remember where you placed an item that may have been missing for a while. You may realize a clear solution on how to fix something around the house that may have been troubling you. You may intuitively connect a body ailment with something you've been eating or doing and realize how to remedy it. You may have a creative idea about how to do something more efficiently at work, an event for the family to do on the weekend or an artistic song or painting. A lot of what you receive will depend on your personality, character and karmic past. Try not to get too consumed in the thought right at that moment but let it float pass and when you've reached the amount of time that you committed yourself to then simply have a pen and paper nearby where you can jot down your ideas.

The more often you practice calmness and stillness, the more profound and creative your ideas will become in time. Not only will creative ideas manifest during your quiet time but you'll continue to carry along your inner calmness with you throughout the day and along with this you'll have creative ideas that come as a result of something you see on TV, the radio, something a friend says or simply something you observe in such a way that you've never noticed before.

A good friend of mine, who is very business-oriented, believes he doesn't have a creative bone in his body. This is only because he has a perception of what creative people are supposed to look like. He thinks that creative people are supposed to be eccentric, wear outlandish clothes and act like hippies or tree huggers. The truth is we are all creative in our own ways. He happens to be creative in business. He is successful at what he does and enjoys the challenge of selling items to people. When a particular strategy he attempts doesn't work, he then has to go back and figure out what he may have said right or wrong, review his presentation, work on his energy, tone and inflection and strengthen his conviction. These are all creative processes.

Additionally, he enjoys wearing professional looking clothing so even his attire selection requires a degree of creativity. He has to select suits that coordinate with his shoes, ties, shirts and handkerchiefs. The key is to channel that creativity into other areas that he is equally passionate about. This is important! Don't try to become something that is not a natural fit for you. In the beginning, you should only try to incorporate creative aspects that are not too far of a stretch from who you are already. In time, you'll be able to stretch out farther but if you totally uproot everything you've been for a lifetime, you'll most likely go through some shell shock with a complete transformation. I'm not saying that it can't be done but depending on your circumstances that may not be the best way to steer the ship in a new direction.

I have a four-year-old son I was trying to teach to ride his bicycle with training wheels. First of all, he's never crashed before so he had this fearless attitude of riding his bike. He was attempting to go down these steep hills at full speed and he didn't even know how to apply his brakes. I had to stay close by him to be able to stop him. I was trying to figure out how can I get him to realize he cannot go that fast on his own when I'm not around without him having to literally crash to learn from experience that you can get hurt. Also, if he wanted to turn his bike in another direction, he would do so by completely turning the handlebars in a 90-degree angle. Of course if you do this then you are going to cause the bike to flip over. Like driving a car, it typically only takes a small change in the wheel to completely change your direction. This should be your approach towards incorporating new creative ideas into your life. Decide which creative ideas are worth pursuing and gradually begin to bring them into action. You'll find in time that every creative idea isn't worth pursuing but some seem to truly resonate with you more greatly. These are the creative ideas you want to make an increased part of who you are.

As I stated earlier, no one truly ever has an original idea. All ideas of science, physics and nature already exist, it's just a matter of who will be first to unravel a mystery or crack the code for a solution to a problem. This is evidenced in the fact that people on opposite sides of the globe could be feverishly working towards the solution to an issue that plagues the world. I, for one, used to do music production. I would have an epiphany in the middle of the night or come up with, what I believed to be, a unique idea. Yet before I could put all the pieces together to bring that song into fruition, I might turn on the radio and hear a new song that is almost the splitting image of the idea I was working on. Likewise, I can't count the times that I did successfully create a song and share with friends or even send out demos to later on hear a song strangely familiar being played in a club. Of course, it would be almost impossible to prove that someone actually took my idea so I had no choice but to accept the fact that the other person's song was the one meant to become popular. Part of nurturing the creative process is to be able to accept ahead of time the notion that what is "right" for you will fall into place at the right time and will bring about the greatest benefit for all.

Spiritual Practice: *Through presence, my intuitive understanding increases leading me to creative pursuits.*

Advisor says...

Practicing creativity when it comes to financial smarts can actually be very fun. We must acknowledge that everyone in their current state is not cut out to be business owners or entrepreneurs. You must be able to make an honest assessment of yourself to determine this. Even if you do decide that you want to take a stab at it, you should accept that it wouldn't be a cakewalk. The majority of small businesses fail within their first year. Of the ones that do survive their first year, the majority of them will be gone within five years. If you do survive the first five years then your success rate increases drastically but there still is no guarantee. Things beyond your control are always prone to happen such as new technology, competition, population shifts, behavioral and perception changes of the customers and any number of unforeseen possibilities.

Therefore, you must do your homework when it comes to pursuing creative ideas related to business and finances. Simply because you may find something unique and interesting doesn't mean other people will. However, you equally shouldn't necessarily let that be a deterrent either. I've seen stories of a simple potter that began making vases and various other sculptures for his own personal pleasure and after receiving great positive feedback from peers, was able to sell an item to a famous celebrity. After that initial sale came more and more offers for his work. Now one of his creations goes for thousands of dollars. Everyone may not have this stroke of fortune but you never know unless you try. In spite of what percentages may suggest about your success, the most absolute and daunting ratio is that you are guaranteed to **not** succeed if you never try. In fact, this has been one of my favorite quotes, *"The greatest risk in life… is never risking anything!"*

Now for the person who may be content in their job but has always had a fancy for another particular venture, I suggest you just start it as a hobby. Anything you enjoy doing, you should do just for the pleasure and satisfaction you receive from it. If you want to go a step further, you can join a local group of people with shared interests or even start a group if there are currently none available. I've seen simple hobbies transform into successful businesses when people realize they are not the only one that is seeking that particular product, service or experience. Where there is a demand, you will always find someone ready to supply. This is the nature of business. The greatest business is one that doesn't feel like work; rather you look forward to immersing yourself in it and never have to count the hours constantly looking at your watch.

For those still seeking even less direct involvement but just want to find creative business expression in other ways then I suggest investing. Of course, you should always first have the necessities in place such as your emergency fund, retirement savings and life insurance. As a quick note on life insurance, everyone should have it! Most people think I must have a spouse, significant debt, kids or the like in order to justify having life insurance. I challenge this notion even if you are wealthy. Think about it. The only thing guaranteed in life is death! This isn't meant to be morbid but it is the only assured truth we have. Everyone will leave this planet sooner or later. Since no one knows when that day will be for him or her, you are essentially gambling. The easiest way out is that you actually do just pass away when your time comes but I've seen people who were wealthy and refused to get life insurance. Instead, of dying they get diagnosed with cancer. Now they have to completely change their lifestyle to deal with this serious medical issue. I've watched families deplete their entire savings and assets struggling to cover medical costs.

If you think you have great health benefits that will cover you in this type of medical issue it would behoove you to think again. You may want to read the fine print again because there are normally lifetime caps on how much they will cover. Also, if you get sick or diagnosed with a serious ailment, that then becomes a precondition that may eliminate you from ever being able to get coverage or at least coverage that you can afford. Now I know a lot of this may become moot with the so-called health care reform but even as we speak there are those seeking to repeal a lot of those measures. Do you really want legislation that is subject to change depending on the very fickle opinions of the public to determine you and your families well being? Not to mention, you'll most likely never be any healthier than what you are today. (Of course, this is for people who are not presently experiencing a major health issue.) The point is that no one is getting younger and even if you remain in great health, the fact that you age each year means the insurance companies are going to charge you more and more for that coverage the older you get.

Life insurance is the same as any other insurance such as your home or vehicle, you may not appreciate the payment but you certainly are glad you have it when you need it. Now tell me what has greater value to you, your car, house or your life? Most cars and homes don't make money but if you're a healthy working person chances are you have a lifetime of opportunity to create wealth. So buy life insurance as young and healthy as possible based on what you can afford before you actually may have a need for it. That way if you do decide to get married, have children or more children, buy a home or multiple homes, start a business etc you won't suddenly be hit with a hefty payment to leverage debt you could've been paying significantly less for had you gotten it earlier. As far as those that are wealthy and may have no debt, you still get to pay pennies on the dollar for what your family will get in return at your passing. It is very simple mathematics. You will typically only pay a fraction in terms of payments compared to the death benefit your family will receive when you're no longer here to generate income. Of course you want to talk to a financial professional to determine the right type of insurance for you and the pros and cons of each. Whole life, term life or combinations of these will vary from person to person. Ok, I'll get off that soapbox for now.

Now for those that do have unique interests then the stock market may be right for you. Most investors go into investing with the mindset of give me a recommendation that will make me a lot of money. This approach is often short-lived because that type of investor has no true interest in the company they've invested in. Not to mention if they see that value fluctuate, they are ready to trade in their chips in a heartbeat. I typically encourage people to invest in companies, products or services that you have some degree of passion or desire to see succeed. If you are into computers then that may be a good place to start. Find companies that are in that industry. Even if your interest is in Hollywood movies, sports, foreign travel, animals or whatever you can dream of there are generally some sort of companies directly engaged in that line of work. Now as a caveat I will warn you that just because you may find that industry interesting doesn't mean that the population does or that it will become a thriving business anytime soon. As always, a lot of factors weigh into the success of a company and many cannot be predicted such as technology, cultural shifts, wars, competition and so forth.

That's why I encourage diversification. In other words, don't put all your eggs in one basket. Take your time to do an internet search, speak with colleagues or an advisor and have someone assist you in drafting up a portfolio of stocks or mutual funds that are in harmony with your interests and passions while ensuring they make good sound financial sense and enjoy!

Financial Tip: *Educate yourself or work with an advisor to help bring your creative ideas to fruition through proper investing.*

Coach says...

Being creative in body begins with accepting and loving yourself as you are! We, unfortunately, live in a society that constantly judges everyone superficially by their appearance, never taking the time to truly get to know people for who they are within. From childhood we learn we are too dark, too pale, too short, too tall, too thin, too big, too pretty, too ugly and so on. Of course these are normally extensions of people's own insecurities being imposed on others. If you were fortunate enough to make it through childhood to become a functioning adult, I say "kudos" to you. However, sometimes these impressions from our past become suppressed and they continue to affect us in our day-to-day lives as adults in the form of lack of confidence, esteem and initiative.

There are studies that show tall men tend to be the ones who are promoted most often in the corporate world. I guess the biases continue to operate even as adults. I suppose this makes sense since a lot of times the tall guys become the athletes and jocks or are merely looked up to simply because you have no choice! ☺ Of course, attractive people continue to get interviews, positions and opportunities not always because of their skill or talent but merely because of their looks. These apparently are the ways of not just the human species but plenty of other animal kingdoms so rather than try to change the game; you have to learn how to play it to win.

You should start by embracing what is unique about you. No matter what your appearance, take solace in the fact that there is no one else in the world that looks like you. Unless of course you have an identical twin… but even then you both still have your own unique personalities so embrace what makes you stand out. Find clothes that compliment your body and figure. If you're not sure what that may be then seek assistance from family, friends or coworkers; preferably people who know how to actually dress themselves and who knows you may help someone else find their passion in life in the process. Part of building self-confidence starts out with being humble enough to know when to ask for help. Regardless of what physical features may be presently beyond your control, you should always be in charge of your personal hygiene. Smell is most significantly linked to memory. So ensuring your body emits a pleasant clean fresh scent should be simple enough. There's no need to overdo it with too heavy perfumes or colognes. Again, if not sure get some feedback from colleagues.

As far as our physical features go, it may take some discipline and time but as they say "you are what you eat." You can be creative in your meal selection by learning to diversify your menu selections. If you are single you can still find a friend or someone ready to take the challenge with you to eat healthier. Obviously, nutritious meals balanced with fresh fruit, vegetables and plenty of water will do the most good. If you have health insurance then speak with a doctor to find out based upon your body's chemistry what food is most appropriate for you and your health. We are not all built the same and therefore our diets should be equally unique.

Also remember your beauty or lack thereof is never an excuse to be an ugly person towards others. Ultimately, this is what people will remember most about you. If you're physically attractive but have a personality offensive to everyone around you then you still won't have very many true friends. People will anxiously await the opportunity to witness your downfall. To be truly loved means that you give love towards all others in equal or greater portion. Lastly, never be afraid to take chances. Depending on what your job may be, if it requires you to be conservative, you can still find other outlets to express your creativity through clothing, hairstyling, tattoos, jewelry or whatever. Love yourself not for superficial reasons but on your ability to know that you are truly a good person and you will exude a magnetism that no one can deny and for those that still may try - do as they say and "shake those haters off!"

Success Skill: *Give yourself a makeover if need be but most importantly embrace who you are and allow your physical appearance to express success!*

"The creative is the place where no one else has ever been. You have to leave the city of your comfort and go into the wilderness of your intuition. What you'll discover will be wonderful. What you'll discover is yourself."

Alan Alda

THE PRINCIPLE OF VISUALIZATION

*"The entrepreneur is essentially a visualizer and an actualizer... He can **visualize** something, and when he visualizes it, he sees exactly how to make it happen."*

Robert L. Schwartz

Coach says...

Successful behaviors and visualization go hand in hand. As you begin to become clearer in your vision of whom you choose to be, you should make **that** your focus and not lose sight of it. If your vision has you dressing a certain way, groomed a certain way and acting a certain way then you should begin to incorporate that into your being. It may feel a little awkward at first if you're stepping outside of your comfort zone but the more consistent you are, the more it'll become second nature to you. It also helps to surround yourself with people who will serve as positive inspiration. If your goal is to become a doctor, then begin to think and act like a doctor and attend lectures, seminars or frequent the places that doctor go. Now just to perspective, what I'm suggesting is that you humbly begin to mold yourself into your vision. This does not mean to impersonate a doctor! Do not try to be something or claim to be something that you are not currently. The point I'm making is that if you are sincere and work towards your vision then surrounding yourself in the right atmosphere will help to keep you focused.

Now it will be a challenge for some people to be able to objectively gauge their strengths and weaknesses. You do not want to become a victim of your own creation. You must realize and always remember that you are NOT your creation rather your creation of yourself stems from your infinite consciousness within. To use an analogy, your consciousness within is like a white canvas. By itself it has the infinite potential to become whatever you paint upon it. The test for a lot of people is that they become so identified with their own painting of themselves, we call this *ego*, that they fall into despair if they are no longer able to keep up a certain image. You should let your image serve you but don't serve your image! If you no longer like the experience you are having or if you begin to see people separating themselves from you then perhaps its time to look in the mirror and reassess what you may have become. If people are being turned off by you, it's not always because they are "haters" it may truly be that you have lost sight of genuineness and have fallen into the trap of becoming self serving.

The same way you can create or modify your image or ego, the same way you can change it at anytime. Practicing presence of mind, the **First Principle**, will help you to be observant and help you develop the self-control to change ways more quickly. As your consciousness evolves, with consistent practice and effort, your ability to control behaviors will strengthen. I've witnessed people totally modify their personalities of stage fright, public speaking, their diets, health practices, exercise routines, style of dress, job performance and reviews through the practice of presence, visualization and preparation.

Now if you have a clear vision of where you're going, where you want to be, have your ego in check and are looking to benefit a greater good than just your own, don't let anything else deter or stop you. Don't let anyone tell you it can't be done. People do sometimes try to impose their own limitations upon others because they are too scared to try. Just remind yourself to not focus on anyone's "negativity" and instead keep your eyes on the prize and take any challenging experience as an opportunity to strengthen your resolve or use it as a learning tool. As they say, there are many ways to skin a cat so never think that one person's help or lack thereof can stop you from achieving your goals. If you are having a difficult time getting through a hurdle then find another way to go over, around or under it. These little tests along the way help to build your character. To be great you must have great character!

Success Skill: *Dare to become the highest vision of yourself! This is not delusion; this is consciously*

choosing to embody the values most important to you!

Advisor says...

When it comes to financial smarts and making investment decisions, it is imperative that you have a vision and know not only **why** you're putting your money in a certain place but also what your **intentions** are for that money. I don't want to get too deep into the history of money, but it is important to recognize why money was created in the first place. People don't really care about money, we care about either an asset (good) such as a home, car, business, clothing, computer etc or we're concerned with access to a resource (service) such as vacations, dining out, movies, sporting events, travel, medical care, charity functions and so forth. Once upon a time people would barter for these goods and services. I'll trade you my pig for a couple of your chickens. The value of an object was determined by its scarcity or upon the degree to which it was able to make your life easier or more enjoyable. Of course, as society evolves, we develop more practical ways of exchanging services since it is not easy to carry animals around with you. So, money became the "legal tender" to exchange value. Money initially had value when it represented something like a precious metal such as gold or silver. Unfortunately, some brilliant people realized this wouldn't be sustainable forever so they essentially removed money's true value by replacing it with nothing other than a "promise" that the government will ensure its value. This change essentially marks the beginning of the end.

Wealthy people, who are much further along in their understanding of money than the average person who doesn't have much of it, learn very quickly that it is not advantageous for them to keep their wealth in money or simply as decimal places in someone's bank. Wealthy people understand that the greatest value of money is in the assets it can represent. In other words, the value of a paper dollar can fluctuate drastically depending on a lot of factors such as the economy, unemployment, how much money is being dumped into it by the government, trade, inflation, taxes and so on. However, true actual assets don't fluctuate as drastically such as a home or business. More importantly, the wealthy try to keep their money in "visionary" vehicles that will grow in value so they always have an asset that can be liquidated if need be. They may keep their money in a business and have the free access to use that money for cars, travel, lodging and so on and then write it off as a business expense thus avoiding or minimizing taxes and the exposure of that dollar to other various costs the average person is hit with daily such as fees, penalties, charges and taxes.

Likewise, it is important for the average working-class person to begin to put their money into their vision. Now this doesn't mean to take your life savings and dump it into a risky business venture. What I am saying is be smart and recognize that you have multiple goals you need to achieve. Hopefully, retiring comfortably and being debt free may be a couple of important ones to you. I recognize that the less money you have, the more challenging it is to diversify your dollars. But you have to establish this mindset and stick to it to the best of your ability. That may mean living a little more frugally and making some sacrifices. Again, I don't want to give specific dollar amounts or percentages because everyone's situation will be unique. However, there are some important must do's that you simply cannot ignore.

First and foremost, work on your savings or emergency savings. Next take advantage of a retirement account. Next, the younger and healthier you are put your defensive strategy into place by obtaining life insurance. Simultaneously, be aware of your credit standing and protect or improve that as needed. These items become your foundation. If you ignore these essentials, then you put your future well-being and livelihood at risk to unforeseen circumstances. If you don't have a strong foundation, then your vision may come crumbling down around you and you have to start from scratch if you're lucky. In a worse case scenario, you may find yourself in a hole you can never dig your way out from.

Now from there you need to focus on growing your assets. I try not to focus on money because money like I said has no true value of its own. You need to program yourself to start thinking in terms of assets. Your assets again will be some form of good or service. This will help you to better identify appropriate investment vehicles for your money, timelines and goals. Too many people get caught up in the trap of having investments with the only purpose of making more money and because your vision is unclear you get trapped in not knowing when to invest or when to take your money out. People watch the stock markets go up and down everyday and it has no real meaning or value because it's all just numbers. But if you specifically know that this investment here is for retirement then unless you're retiring you shouldn't touch it. You should only use that money in emergencies of the sort in degree of unemployment, major health issue or something catastrophic. Otherwise, you're changing the vision for those dollars and likewise the fruition of that vision.

So, to clarify, once you have all the appropriate investment vehicles in place for a strong foundation then decide how you intend for other dollars to be utilized in terms of assets. If you know you want to take a vacation then focus, prepare and visualize that vacation and invest your dollars accordingly based upon your timeframe. Depending upon your timeframe, your level of risk should coincide. Speak with a professional to discuss this with you. If you plan to buy a home, establish your timeframe, how much you can invest, how often and your risk level. This should be your approach towards every investment decision – college savings, healthcare, home purchase, a family move, change of career, business startup and so on. Once you have a fairly good grasp of these investment smarts, then you may learn how to keep your dollars invested in businesses to minimize other tax burdens and liquidation repercussions.

Financial Tip: *Put your dollars to use in helping to manifest your vision!*

Yogi says...

As you begin to gain some greater insight, knowledge and understanding of the potential and the feasibility of your creative ideas, you then begin to visualize yourself doing what you dream. This is a crucial step! All things begin with choice. Ideas stem from nowhere. They simply manifest by the desire of the consciousness within you. The "building material" needed to transform that idea into an experience begins with your visualization. The greater your clarity, vision and consistency, the more energy you put behind your ideas and the experience will follow more quickly and to a greater degree.

If you only occasionally visualize an idea or simply sit around waiting for it to come to you then the less likely you are to experience it. I can't say it enough… we are creators! First, we create visually through an idea.   Ideas are subtle but they most certainly have creative energy. Most of us have not developed the ability to read another's thoughts but we've all probably experienced a time when we've picked up on another's energy as soon as they came into the room.   Thoughts are energy. We've all heard the expression that some people "wear their emotions on their sleeves."   Well, emotions stem from the thoughts or internal dialogue we communicate to ourselves. Our egos, personalities and perception influence what we tell ourselves which are normally based upon past experience. From there our thoughts influence our emotions and we all, to greater or lesser degree, display these emotions and energy through our faces, posture and body language. Of course, once our emotions begin to influence our body language, we often will lose our awareness and our actions are then being driven by our emotions.

This is why the practice of **"Presence"** is first and foremost. The more we are able to practice presence the more control of our egos and perception we gain. The greater control we have of our perception, the greater control we have of our internal dialogue, which is nothing more than our thoughts, and we can from there keep better check of our emotions and hence body language and actions.   It all works like an avalanche. Our perception is like the wind. The wind of our perception shakes and vibrates our thoughts, which is like the still snowflakes on the mountaintop. As our thoughts vibrate with energy, they become the emotion, which shakes the entire snowbed, and emotions out of control become the avalanche, which is very hard to stop. It essentially causes havoc until the energy dissipates of its own.

What we are striving for, through visualization, is to control the energy and direct the "snowball" to become a controlled "avalanche" that we use to create good and the things we seek to experience. This is the same way water is used in conjunction with dams to generate electricity. So, our thoughts come from an unmanifested state of being and through visualization they begin to take form initially in our own minds.   The greater our focus and the more consistent we entertain the vision, the more "solid" it becomes and begins to manifest itself first through our own bodies. Our thoughts and visions gain greater magnitude through our words, which vibrate on a grosser level and ultimately our actions become what we experience through the five senses.   However, it doesn't stop here. What we express in physical form through our words and actions also influence the objects and most importantly the people around us. Depending upon the energy you are putting out, your actions towards others will either impact them in a positive way and they feel more attracted to you or you influence others in a negative way, and we repel them.

Nowadays, there is a lot of talk about "haters." A hater is essentially someone that doesn't want you to succeed for no other reason than they are simply jealous. While it may be true to some degree that these people may exist, they honestly do not have any power to thwart your goals. More importantly, if you're experiencing a lot of "haters" around you then it is because you are attracting them to you! Remember, your thoughts are things and have energy. If you have a core belief that people don't like you, think you're stuck up, are jealous of you etc, then that is exactly what you're going to attract or rather **create** for yourself as an experience. We all must understand the world is a very big place full of an infinite amount of possibilities. Your thoughts are energy and the energy you put out draws you to precisely the "like kind" of energy.

So, guess what? There are no absolute truths in this world of relativity. If you believe the world is full of racists, then that will be your experience relatively speaking. If you believe people are inherently selfish, then that will be your experience. What you believe doesn't make it absolutely true. It just makes it **relatively** true for you! If you want to change your relative experience, then you have to look in the mirror and start with yourself. It doesn't mean that racism and selfishness cease to exist in the world, it just means that you relatively changed your belief system and hence your experience. Hopefully, you just had a light bulb moment. If not, let me stress this point again. There are no absolute truths in this world. This relative world will never be completely peaceful or completely evil. It will never be completely rich or completely destitute. It is only relative to the individual experience. As an example, if I gave $20 to a homeless person, I may have just made his or her day! That may be the biggest handout anyone has ever given them. They may have only been looking to get a sandwich but now with this excess money they have a lot more options and for that moment they may feel rich. However, if I give $20 to someone who is used to getting $100 tips or makes thousands of dollars in a day, they may feel insulted. That $20 won't even get them a decent meal at the restaurants they may frequent. The only things "absolute" in these two scenarios is the $20 but the experience is drastically different based upon that person's internal dialogue. Their belief system is influencing their thoughts, emotions and thus experience.

It is a fact that the person who is grateful for every experience that comes to them puts himself or herself in a greater position to attract greater riches because they are already telling themselves that the "little" experiences are already great! The first goal is to try to change your own thought. The simplest way to change your thought is to change your internal dialogue. The simplest way to change your internal dialogue is to change your perception. The simplest way to change your perception is to merely redirect your attention away from the "haters" and place it on the positive people. For every hater there has to be a friend, loved one or supporter in your life. Haters are like controversy.

If you're driving down the road and you see an accident on the side of the road it is very tempting to focus your attention on the accident. Of course, commonsense tells us if we're not looking straight ahead at the road, we are more likely to steer out of our lane, off the road or perhaps get into an accident ourselves. This is why police officers are trained to be aware of the traffic behind them and to park their vehicles a certain way. They know from experience how many accidents occur because of people taking their eyes off the road or being drawn in by the flashing lights. Haters work the same way. If you focus on them then you are of your own accord taking your eyes off the road and allowing them to distract you from your goals. It may take a little discipline, but you do have the power to not get distracted and to focus on your path. The more focused on your goals you are, the more you focus on the positive people and events in your life; the more the "haters" will fade away and of course this merely strengthens your perception, thoughts, internal dialogue and hence your words, actions and experience. It all goes around full circle.

So again, use your intuition to begin to make your creative thoughts more concrete by narrowing them down to a select few and begin breathing life into those thoughts by focusing on them frequently. It may help you to cut out pictures from a magazine, download them off the Internet, save them as screensavers or put a poster up if a visual aid helps you. You can put up positive words on your bathroom mirror, so you see them in the morning or put your goals on the refrigerator, front door as you go out to work in the morning etc. The more you practice presence, the greater your creative thoughts and vision will become so that in time you won't even need a visual aid. Begin by focusing on maybe just one creative idea. Then share it by expressing the thought in words to people you know will be supportive. Then begin to speak it with greater conviction. Then take those ideas and words and begin to put them into action. We'll talk more about taking action in the **Fifth Principle** but first we need to clarify *principle of purpose* in step four.

Spiritual Practice: *My life is a reflection of my thoughts. By having a clear vision for myself I will create the life I choose!*

"I would **visualize** *things coming to me. It would just make me feel better. Visualization works if you work hard. That's the thing. You can't just visualize and go eat a sandwich."*

Jim Carrey

THE PRINCIPLE OF PURPOSE

"I know of no more encouraging fact than the unquestionable ability of man to elevate his life by a conscious endeavor."

Henry David Thoreau

Yogi says...

As you develop your routine of spending some quiet time alone, nurturing your conscious presence, developing your creative ideas, filtering out the ones you seek to manifest and begin visualizing them as your reality, now is the time to bring purpose to all of your endeavors! Having a purpose gives meaning to our lives and everything we do. It is the difference between ordinary men and those who become great. It's like eating bread and water to simply satisfy hunger or enjoying a well-balanced four-star meal at a beach resort. Without having a purpose, your life will most likely remain mediocre. So, what is meant by purpose? A purpose is a noble cause, a vision, a mission or statement that defines who you are and what you are about.

Your purpose can be as simple or grand as you like but it should be bigger than just yourself. Saying I want to be rich or I want to be a basketball player is not a purpose. It doesn't mean a rich person or basketball player do not have a purpose. If a rich person assists others through philanthropic efforts, then that may be their purpose to help other people achieve their dreams through business. However, getting rich in itself is not a purpose. Likewise, becoming a famous basketball player in itself is not a purpose. Professional basketball attracts millions of fans because it binds an entire city, state and sometimes a nation in achieving a goal. It exemplifies the possibilities of success from playing as a team and cohesive unit. It entertains people in clutching moments of excitement, anxiety, and stress but also the jubilation of winning. If your only goal is to get rich from playing basketball, chances are you will never become one of the great ones. However, if you understand that your skills make you unique and you become a symbol as the person who overcomes tribulation and plays not just for themselves but to entertain the masses, then you have found a **purpose** to play and that will assuredly make you great and remembered!

So, saying I want to improve other people's lives, feed the hungry, fight poverty or entertain people *is* a purpose. When seeking to find or establish your purpose, you should begin by exploring those creative ideas that resonate with you the most. Try to find where in society there is a need and make it your mission to fill that void. Try to give life to a purpose that has the ability to outlive you. None of us are promised tomorrow, so wouldn't it be great to know someone has taken up the mantle and continued your life's work for you. That is the best way to be remembered, as someone who stood for an idea larger than you.

Don't get discouraged if your purpose isn't immediately clear. This is why I recommend first exploring your creative ideas, visualizing yourself expressing them and as you begin to test the waters, your purpose will come into focus in due time. Sometimes you may never realize what your purpose is but by simply seeking to help others in the best way you can through your creative ideas and to your best ability, your purpose will find you! All wealthy, prominent and successful people who have had significant impacts upon the world all had a purpose to their work. They had a vision that started as a creative idea, which is normally "crazy" to everyone else, but they believed in that idea and pursued it. Sometimes you may be the only person who understands where you're coming from but don't fret over that. If you see a need and you're seeking to help others, then you will achieve your goals with the right amount of determination.

Now a lot of people still may not be clear on the idea of purpose. Oprah Winfrey has stated in many of her interviews that she enjoys speaking with guests, asking questions, interviewing them, teaching people in the audience and learning from others. Obviously, these are things she does very well hence her tremendous success. However, she states that her **purpose** is to spread love. So, all of the work she does is under the mission to spread love to all. That is a great universal purpose that everyone can use. After 25 years of her show, she has decided to retire from interviewing but has evolved to now owning her own network. This is a key factor in having a purpose versus just seeking to have a business or do a job. When you have a clear purpose, you can transition into many other avenues in life, doing many different things and yet still be fulfilling your purpose.

Most of us become attached and identified with our jobs, titles or businesses. We see ourselves as doctors, lawyers, engineers, mechanics, teachers, barbers, advisors, legislators and so forth. But when we view ourselves this way it limits our potential for growth and transformation. A lot of people become saddened if they are forced to retire, if they have an accident that somehow inhibits them from now doing their job or if they are laid off. Now if instead of seeing yourself as your job function, you focus on a higher purpose it gives you the freedom, the creativity and the vision to better see your next move.

Instead of saying I'm a doctor, say my **purpose** is to help heal others. So, if the day comes when you've either aged or physically can no longer perform as a doctor, you can easily transition to other lines of work that still allow you to fulfill your purpose as a "healer." You may teach or train other doctors, you may start a non-profit, you may speak at seminars, give radio interviews, start a blog or whatever that still allows you to heal others.

Instead of just being a lawyer, determine that your purpose is to ensure justice for all. Again, there are many ways to do this than just in a courtroom. Instead of simply being an engineer recognize that you can be a visionary, someone who seeks to improve people's lives, through technology or whatever your specialty may be. Instead of simply cutting heads as a barber, make it your purpose to brighten people's day. Educate them on ways to improve their appearance and hygiene. Think of yourself as a "self esteem booster" and make that your purpose and you'll soon discover many new avenues for you to assist people in this way. Instead of being a mechanic, make it your purpose to educate people, improve their way of life, simplify daily routines or processes, be imaginative and think of ways to improve on current systems or mechanisms. Good mechanics make some of the best inventors. Create something worth patenting!

Don't just be a teacher collecting a check. Make it your purpose to groom and nurture children or young adults. J.K. Rowling, the author of the Harry Potter series, also the richest woman billionaire in the world, wanted to help end child illiteracy. She went through a rough divorce and became a single mother. At one point she had to survive off of welfare. She knew since a child that she enjoyed writing but never knew what to write about. Then one day in her twenties on a train ride, the idea of a boy wizard popped into her mind and it all just suddenly made sense. She may not realize it but I'm certain that peaceful train ride put her into a moment of **presence,** and through that tranquil clarity, she was able to receive the creative ideas to formulate a book story that would become an empire.

Her publisher thought children's books wouldn't sell and particularly thought young boys wouldn't want to read books written by a woman, but they were wrong. She had the courage though to see beyond just the benefits of a successful book and understood that her **purpose** was to make reading fun and educate children in the process. These are a couple examples of two extremely successful people who didn't just seek to get rich but breathe life into their **purpose** and surpassed any success they could have imagined.

Spiritual Practice: *I will utilize my uniqueness to my advantage to find or create a purpose to assist others in a way that only I can do!*

Advisor says...

Your finances are like a body of water. You can either let them sit there stagnant used only with the intent of your own benefit and like most stagnant bodies of water they eventually won't even be any good to you or you can channel your finances to become like a raging river helping to sustain many others in the process. Giving purpose to your finances empowers them to better your life and others, generate ideas and make dreams come true. This begins with financial smarts, understanding money, learning how to optimize your dollars and to give purpose to your financial decisions.

I'll continue throughout this book to reiterate the importance of having a solid financial foundation before spreading your wings to venture into other options with your money. But if you do have your needs met, bills covered and are looking for ways to grow your assets then it is imperative to first be clear in your purpose. Again, if you're only looking for ways to make money then you may be sucked into a money-making scheme that is just that – a scheme! I won't suggest that there aren't

The Golden Egg

reading fun and educate children in the process. These are a couple examples of two extremely successful people who didn't just seek to get rich but breathe life into their **purpose** and surpassed any success they could have imagined.

Spiritual Practice: *I will utilize my uniqueness to my advantage to find or create a purpose to assist others in a way that only I can do!*

Advisor says...

Your finances are like a body of water. You can either let them sit there stagnant used only with the intent of your own benefit and like most stagnant bodies of water they eventually won't even be any good to you or you can channel your finances to become like a raging river helping to sustain many others in the process. Giving purpose to your finances empowers them to better your life and others, generate ideas and make dreams come true. This begins with financial smarts, understanding money, learning how to optimize your dollars and to give purpose to your financial decisions.

I'll continue throughout this book to reiterate the importance of having a solid financial foundation before spreading your wings to venture into other options with your money. But if you do have your needs met, bills covered and are looking for ways to grow your assets then it is imperative to first be clear in your purpose. Again, if you're only looking for ways to make money then you may be sucked into a money-making scheme that is just that – a scheme! I won't suggest that there aren't

72

industries and legitimate opportunities that haven't yet been discovered or are on the precipice of taking off but if it doesn't really make sense to you then it is probably best that you stay away from businesses where you don't understand the purpose. Warren Buffett, the richest investor ever and one of the top three richest people in the world, doesn't invest in businesses that he doesn't understand. Believe it or not but one of those "businesses" he doesn't understand is property. So according to him he stays away from it. This proved to be a wise choice for him, and he avoided potential significant losses the majority of the nation experienced with the most recent real estate collapse.   I'm not suggesting that he never loses money but at least you are more likely to accept a loss when it's due to a reason you can grasp. If you understand the factors that contributed to the loss, then you're in a better position to determine if you want to "weather the storm" or bail ship. You also gain the advantage of better understanding how to recover the loss.

Another important factor in understanding the purpose of your financial decisions is the reality that it takes money to make money in this world we live in. You may or may not like it but until the ways of the world change it behooves you to understand how to play the game in order to survive. A lot of people seem to have this impression that there are legitimate ways to make tons of money without any significant investment. I hate to disappoint but again this really just isn't the way it works. Even the Federal Reserve has to spend money to make money! They have to pay employees, constantly upgrade manufacturing processes, improve security and software, fight counterfeiters and improve the science behind legal tender. People seem to want everything for nothing. Great returns with no risk; sorry but it just doesn't exist. Laziness and lack of effort will never produce magnificent rewards.

The most assured way to nurture financial prosperity is to fully understand your purpose in any decision. You may think it's a great business to print t-shirts but if your only purpose is to express your creativity then your t-shirt printing "business" may only prove to be a hobby. If on the other hand, you're clear that you seek to combine your creativity with the purpose of providing t-shirts to sporting teams, family reunions, church organizations, local businesses, nightclubs and so forth then clearly defining that purpose will resonate with your potential customers. They'll be much more likely sold on your quest to fill a need than simply your desire to show off your artwork. Without a clearly defined purpose you're more likely to end up as the "starving artist." Most corporations have a mission statement; this essentially is their **purpose** for existence and why they are in business. Focusing on that goal keeps your vision more clearly defined and you're better able to fulfill the needs of others.

Between 2007 and 2009, a lot of leading financial investment firms and banks we would've never thought would be out of business did just that; go out of business! They were forced to file bankruptcy or to be acquired by other companies. What was the cause of their downfall? They lost sight of their purpose! These companies got greedy and began focusing only on the profit motive. They were no longer concerned about serving the customer. They were no longer concerned about being innovative and creative. They forgot about their mission statement. If you're not continuously working towards your purpose, then you're most likely going in the wrong direction. Unfortunately, the downfall of many of these companies meant the customer ended up carrying the burden. The government stepped in for some and decided these institutions were too big to fail. They may have been right but the companies that were able to survive were the ones that had to go back to the drawing board, redefine their purpose and begin to try to regain the trust of their customers.

Financial Tip: *I will not fall into the trap of chasing money. I will give purpose to my financial decisions to bring fruition to my goals.*

Coach says...

There are a lot of wealthy people in this world who do not have a clearly defined purpose. Unfortunately, I do not have any scientific polls or data to back this claim, but I would dare say these individuals are in the minority. Often times, these people either inherited money from a relative, hit the lottery or just were the benefactors of pure dumb luck. Depending on how much they may have amassed, they may even be able to sustain it till the end of their lives. However, if you were able to look at their bankbooks you would clearly see that their fortune is diminishing as opposed to growing. Perhaps that person's parents started a successful business and understood the purpose of their work but if the "newbie" hasn't defined a purpose for himself or herself and if they don't have someone with the financial smarts to help protect their assets, then their wealth may prove to be very short lived.

Having a purpose to your investment decisions begins with having a purpose behind your behaviors. Successful people nurture and practice successful behaviors in order to not only protect their wealth but to find ways for it to prosper. You will never have the experience of success by simply wishing for it. You must discipline your behaviors to breed success. Even people who hit the lottery or sweepstakes didn't simply have someone knock on their door to hand them a check they had to at least take action to purchase the winning ticket, complete a form, purchase a product or enter the contest. These lucky individuals may have "struck gold" but if they don't educate themselves on how to protect their assets, make smart decisions and set goals then their wealth won't likely make it pass one generation.

This is a competitive world we live in, but truth be told the person next to you isn't your competition. You are your own competition! Success doesn't necessarily have to do with you being better than the next person or company; it has everything to do with you being the best you can be. This should be your metric. I acknowledge it can be helpful to glance over from time to time to see what others may be doing to get ahead but the grass will often appear to be greener on the other side. The person that may appear to be surpassing everyone may be bending the rules or flat out breaking the law. Need I mention Enron, Bernie Madoff or a host of athletes and entertainers who think they are above the rules or laws of the land who come crashing back to earth in a great ball of fire?

The point isn't to pick at his or her misfortune but to stress the truth that no one attains anything worth having without earning it! Even the examples of the lottery winner or stroke of good fortune are the result of that person's good karma. Perhaps the "planets were aligned" properly for that person in the moment of time but if they haven't developed the proper character, wisdom and behaviors then it won't last.

So, what are the most effective behaviors for success? Well, it starts with a good consciousness, clarity of thought and a refined vision. Good character, discipline, time management and integrity are important as well but when you have a noble purpose for your efforts then these other qualities seem to fall into place. When you've found the proper purpose that truly resonates with you then you'll find there's no need to cheat to get ahead. You don't have to make yourself do anything because you enjoy doing it. If anything, you'll have to pull yourself away from it, so you don't neglect your other responsibilities in life. Your character tends to shine because you feel good about yourself and it's clearly evident to those around you that you love what you do. You will never have to jeopardize your integrity when you stay focused on your purpose. If you lose sight of your purpose and begin to believe that money "trumps" all then you will sacrifice your integrity and your "success" will soon be lost as well.

Success Skill: *Great success is achieved with great purpose. True lasting prosperity is never given… it is earned!*

"Men who have attained things worth having in this world have worked while others idled, have persevered when others gave up in despair, have practiced early in life the valuable habits of self-denial, industry, and **singleness of purpose***. As a result, they enjoy in later life the success so often erroneously attributed to good luck."*

Glenville Kleiser

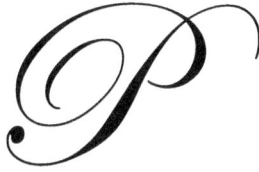

THE PRINCIPLE OF CONCENTRATION

*"The difference in men does not lie in the size of their hands, nor in the perfection of their bodies, but in this one sublime ability of **concentration**: to throw the weight with the blow, to live an eternity in an hour."*

Elbert Hubbard

Coach says...

Concentrate the mind and the body shall follow. Developing and nurturing successful behaviors towards creating prosperity requires discipline and daily focus. Whether you're seeking to improve your physical health, budget the home expenses, get a promotion, start a business or expand your services, they all will require concentrated effort on your part as well as the concentration of any other vital players such as employees. Individual concentration requires self-discipline and self-control and is difficult enough but trying to get others to concentrate requires leadership by example and is much harder. Unfortunately, when it comes to good employees, they tend to be the number one most difficult asset to acquire and maintain. Plenty of people are willing to take a job to collect a paycheck but many won't be qualified and have the right work ethic. Even if they meet those two requirements, they may not buy into the company vision, feel adequately compensated or have the commitment to see success achieved.

All good leaders are most effective when they are able, through their personal concentration, to define a goal and then communicate that goal to a team. However, if you are not leading this charge by example, if you are unfocused or come across as "scattered brain" then no one is going to follow your desires simply because you said so. Strengthening your concentration takes conscious effort and willpower. It is beneficial to have your body and mind in harmony. A tired or exhausted body will cause the mind to drift. Likewise, a fatigued mind will keep the body from feeling vital and strong. In fact, most successful skills, that you may not already possess, will begin with your ability to concentrate. Whether you are looking to learn how to dance, speak a new language, improve public speaking, inspire others or pursue your dreams, your degree of success will be greatly influenced by your degree of concentration.

So how can someone improve his or her concentration? There are many techniques to help one to focus. Granted, there will be times in everyone's life where extenuating circumstances seem to usurp our attention. If you are going through relationship drama, swamped at work, behind on bills or experiencing health issues, it will be extremely challenging to simply block out these other matters and concentrate on one thing. This is why concentration cannot just be a random attempt every now and then. You must get in the practice of taking some personal "me" time everyday to advance your concentration abilities. There will always be things in life demanding your attention but if you don't make it a habit to reserve a specific amount of time daily to just be alone with your thoughts then life's circumstances will always impede your ability to concentrate. Make up your mind now that in order to improve your quality of life, and thus the people around you as well, you must insist that you have the opportunity to be a little "selfish" by finding time to be alone.

This advice goes for spouses with children particularly! Both spouses, regardless to what financial role they play in the relationship, deserve some time to maintain their sanity. If husband and wife are playing traditional roles where the husband works to make a living, then he deserves some time when he comes home to either transition from the work day or to be able to be alone before going to bed. Likewise, if mom takes care of the children all day then she deserves some time away from the kids to soak in the bath or do whatever she needs to replenish. I don't mean this in an egotistical way, but we are all the "centers" of our universes. If our light flickers out, then we are no good to anyone else around us. A stressed out and exhausted mom or dad, husband or wife, isn't beneficial to their spouse or their children. So, it is essential to be able to recoup vital mental energy and vitality in order to be effective in our lives. Life isn't a race; it's a marathon. If you intend to cross the "finish line" of prosperity, then concentrated effort along with moments of repose are critical to achievement.

Success Skill: *I will respect my body giving it time to replenish. Prosperity can only be achieved through balance of concentration and relaxation.*

Yogi says...

Under the first principle of presence our goal is to essentially wipe away all outer distractions by relaxing our body, minds and spirit. Upon being able to find this inner stillness, we become able to tap into all potential energy. As we nurture our intuitive creative ideas, strengthen our vision and define our purpose, we enter the stage where we begin to concentrate all of our energy into specific goals. Every artist or athlete knows the importance of concentration related to their ability to perform at great levels. There are numerous metaphors to paint this picture as well. A raging river harmlessly passes over the rock bed but if you steadily apply one drop of water to the surface of a rock, that water in time will wear down the rock or any other tough substance. If you press your flat hand against a tightly held piece of paper it is difficult to break through it but if you point one focused finger, then you easily break through the paper. Concentration is equivalent to sharpening your blade to a razor's edge and honing all of your energy into one point!

Likewise, concentration is essential to centering our being, focusing our attention, achieving goals and living prosperously. Once we've achieved the greatest presence our attention allows, we can then begin to concentrate on one particular item at a time. The key in being able to manifest prosperity is the connection between your concentration and your will power. Your will power actually starts in the mind and becomes energy in the body. When you begin to concentrate on one idea with consistency, you literally begin to breathe life into that idea. The reason a lot of people fail to materialize their thoughts and desires is because they don't focus on their goal continuously until it manifests. We too often behave "flighty" and when things don't fall into our laps, we move on to the next desire. Yet had you stuck to it a little longer, you may have achieved that very goal.

This is the importance of why I laid out these principles in this particular order. As we practice presence we begin to tap into an infinite storehouse of potential. The more often we do this, the more our intuition strengthens. Our intuition will guide us to the most suitable creative ideas. As we begin to sift through those ideas and visualize the ones that resonate with us most greatly, we begin to identify our unique purposes. Once we've identified our purpose, we can then begin to concentrate on that vision with single focus. Our willpower strengthens as we wake up every day seeking to manifest that purpose.

There have been scientific studies on the brain to try to understand the link between our thoughts and our bodies. Scientists can examine the brain with the proper equipment to actually observe the neurons firing. When a person is asked to move their finger, a neuron fires at the top of the brain. The test also showed that even when the subject didn't actually move their finger but simply imagined or visualized moving their finger, that part of the brain still showed the neuron firing. Scientists naturally asked, "What is causing the neuron to fire if there is no actual movement"? The answer seems to be the person's choice of will. They believe that through sheer choice the "will" of the consciousness reflected in the brain does the work to create the desired result.

So, the question remains "how do we use the will to materialize things"? The answer is concentration! Concentration is the manifestation of the will repeatedly choosing the same desire over and over again until the experience is produced. What made Michael Jordan such a great basketball player? He repeatedly chose, visualized, concentrated and willed himself to manifest the experience of winning. Obviously, the degree of that person's success will be impacted by many variables but ultimately the level of concentration is foremost. The same applies for all successful athletes, performers, musicians and so forth.

Everyone knows Tiger Woods past performance as one of the greatest golf players ever. No doubt if you've ever seen him play you would know his concentration was impeccable. However, after he endured the scandal of his marriage issues being played out in the public, he finally decided to return to golf. Try as he might, his performance on the field was not easily regained. Clearly, none of us can get inside Tiger's head but if I were a gambling man, I would put my money on the fact that although he was trying with all his will, he couldn't get his concentration level to the point it needed to be. This is understandable considering all the controversy that surrounded him. If he desires to get back to his previous levels of success, he will have to regain that essential degree of concentration.

Spiritual Practice: *I will strengthen my concentration abilities to serve me in everything I do.*

Advisor says...

The same rules apply towards financial growth. Obviously, money and finances have no willpower of their own, but your financial decisions and investments can be concentrated to attain specific goals. The more "concentrated" your money is towards a goal, the better it is able to perform and the better you will be able to track its performance. For example, let's say you are a business owner. You are seeking to gain more customers. So, you may start a marketing or advertising campaign. Since your time is valuable and limited, you may decide to acquire the services of another company that specializes in these services. Many of these companies may have package deals that offer print advertising, online advertising, website building, search engine optimization, flyers, mailings, radio, television and so forth. Now the advantage of going with a package deal is that it may save you some money through discount. However, unless that company keeps truly good metrics, it may be difficult to determine what sort of return on investment you're getting.

The variables for success in any sales process begin with the funnel analogy. The large open end of the funnel is the general public, which consists of theoretically an infinite number of potential customers. The other small end of the funnel is an actual paid customer who purchased your product or service. The goal is to get as many potential clients in on the front end of the funnel. As they go through the sales process, many will fall out for one reason or another. They either lost interest, went to a competitor, changed their mind, weren't convinced of your product, didn't truly have the need, couldn't afford it or a number of other possible reasons. The important part is to be able to identify where you are losing the potential customers and for what reason. This can only be achieved by smartly separating the "stop points," keeping good metrics and concentrating on the areas that appear to be the most difficult.

The truth is no matter what your product or service is, it isn't going to appeal to everyone. So immediately you need to try to "predict" what type of customer will you appeal to mostly. Some of these answers will be obvious. If you're trying to sell the Bible to Moslems, chances are you're going to have a difficult time with that sale but if you have identified the right target audience that makes initial contact with them much easier. If you have a very expensive product then clearly you wouldn't want to target lower income neighborhoods. Many of these don't take a genius to figure out but many others are subtler. Large corporations actually have departments whose only purpose is to find out the psychology of what makes their customers buy. They study everything down to race, gender, age group, religious beliefs, economic status and other factors. In fact, there are more and more companies surfacing whose only job is to appeal to these corporations with new technology to help them identify their demographics. Already on the market are cameras that actually scan people's eyes to see what products catch their attention in malls, how long they stare at them and even examine their facial reactions. Some people feel this borders on the line of privacy invasion but you can't deny this is concentrated focus at its finest!

Likewise, I recommend to individuals and businesses to "concentrate" your financial decisions to know and understand why a particular dollar is being spent this or that way, what are the metrics to examine that dollar's usage, how do you measure success or failure and when have we achieved our goal. Whether it is a business expansion or a personal investment, these are variables you should keep in mind to know how to best utilize your dollars. In the investment world, this is known as diversification. Some people prefer diversifying their investments in order to minimize the risk. If you are a gambler, then the best analogy is like playing the roulette table. The more numbers and/or colors you put your money on, the greater your chances at winning. Likewise, since most of us have limited funds, it minimizes your potential returns as well since you have less money to put in your investment options.

On the opposite end of the spectrum, you have investors who only buy stocks because they prefer to "concentrate" their dollars into specific companies they believe in. The advantage is if that company does in deed perform well, then their rewards are more significant. Likewise, there is greater risk because if that company fails then you've most likely seen your investment disappear as well. Diversification and concentration both have their pros and cons in the business and investment world. If you are a new investor with limited funds, then diversification is most likely best for you. If you're somewhere in the middle, then a combination of the two is probably most suitable. Lastly, if you have significant funds to use and have the time to do your homework, then concentrating your dollars into specific business ventures may prove to be your greatest option. Again, you want to sit down with a professional to serve as a sounding board to ensure you're taking the best strategy.

Financial Tip: *I will begin to concentrate my financial assets into clearly defined goals.*

*"**Concentration** is the factor that causes the great discrepancy between men and the results they achieve... the difference in their power of calling together all the rays of their ability and concentrating on one point."*

Orison Swett Marden

THE PRINCIPLE OF ACTION

*"Take time to deliberate; but when the time for **action** arrives, stop thinking and go in!"*

Napolean Bonaparte

Yogi says...

So... are you ready to snatch the pebble, grasshopper? This was the challenge presented by Master Po to young Caine in the 70's movie "Kung Fu." When Caine was able to successfully snatch the pebble from his master, his training was complete and there was nothing left for him to learn at that particular leg of his journey. Likewise, everything you take from this book, other readings, experiences and life in general are meant to help prune you to grow and become more than what you were previously. All things begin with choice and end in deed. In the process of choosing, we entertain thoughts, utilize our wills to act in an effort to produce a specific outcome or result as an experience. Depending upon that outcome and what we experience, we may choose to act again to change or modify that experience. We call this "reacting" when it is in direct response to an experience or someone else's action.

We must come to understand that even when we are reacting, we are still "acting" because we are making a choice. Most of us, however, tend to react with clouded judgment based upon our feelings about a particular experience, which is why we must always remember principle number one – *practice presence!* When you are able to maintain your presence, state of awareness, at all times even in the midst of "unpleasant" experiences then you are better able to think clearly and make the best choices on how to create a better outcome. It serves you to be able to understand what an experience may be telling you and how to best address it. Every experience, even bad ones, has the potential to benefit you even if it is simply a learning experience.

The greatest "disservice" done unto people by Law of Attraction proponents is the idea that you can have everything you want by applying zero effort or by attracting it all to you without having to apply yourself. This is a fallacy people! The bad part is I think most people already instinctively know this, but we want to believe that there is an easier to have everything. The truth is there is an easier way but it's not the opposite extreme of not taking any action at all. The key is in taking the proper, smart action and becoming more efficient. I equate this whole notion of "no effort" to the latest diet fad. People who are not happy with their weight want the latest sensation to make them fit and trim without having to change their behaviors or work for it. We want to continue to lie on the couch, eat everything we want, not exercise and yet still watch the pounds fall off on their own. So, we'll actually spend money every time someone comes along and tells us they found the "secret" on how to achieve this goal and gullible people fall for it everyday!

Even the God of the universe took "action" in creating it. Saying, "Let there be light!" requires an act of will and energy. We may not recognize it, but we are made in the same image to be able to create through choice, will and energy. These are nothing more than subtler forms of **action**! Think about this for a moment because it is a very important detail. Can you name one thing in physical existence that is able to impact its environment or even exist without some degree of action? Energy is transformed through action. The moon acts upon the earth through gravity. In fact, every "body of mass" has a gravitational pull upon other bodies of mass. It is impossible to live without action. Work, walking, sitting and even sleeping all requires action. Every moment our heart beats is an action. Our hearts must beat to circulate blood. Our lungs must act to absorb oxygen and emit toxins. Our brains, digestive systems, neurological systems and so forth all are continuously acting. Fortunately, these processes don't require our conscious effort, but they are actions nonetheless. So how can we possibly believe that "attracting" prosperity doesn't require action? A lot of Law of Attraction advocates may be upset with me for countering a major part of their "philosophy" by exposing these false notions that we can have it all without action. I'll stress again the difference here is in reprogramming what we intuitively know to be true already – we are not "attractors" we are **creators!** To create... you must act!

Now I will give some allowance that as you evolve in your understanding of metaphysics, your "action" can become much subtler and yet still be very effective. As I stated earlier, you must first learn to effectively use the Laws of Nature in order to later on come to know how you can bend the laws. This, unfortunately, will not happen in a matter of days, weeks or most likely even months as many may suggest. In order to truly be able to affect the very nature of matter down to the molecules and atoms, one must have an extreme degree of concentration. This concentration will only come about when you are able to unite with the subtlest consciousness behind even your thoughts. As long as you identify with the restless thoughts, you haven't yet developed the ability to see the true nature of thought and energy and thus will not be able to manipulate them through sheer will. Since this is beyond the scope of this book, I won't dive too deeply into that subject matter but know that your effective action is imperative to creating prosperity.

A lot of people act simply from emotion or habit. You must learn to strengthen your willpower and know that every action you take is a result of your choosing and not simply a reaction to a situation. Weak individuals act from habit and this is unthinking will. "Thinking will" is when we choose how to act from careful consideration. "Dynamic will" is when, through great presence of mind, we develop the ability to concentrate all of our energies to manifest specific goals of our choosing.

Spiritual Practice: *I will use my concentrated intelligence to act smartly!*

Advisor says...

Another false belief we must shatter is the idea that money makes money. Money in and of itself does not make more money. This is not the same as saying "It takes money to make money!" For the most part, I'll agree with that statement. But thinking that money makes money is a misperception. The truth is that ideas in action make money. Now I know some will immediately argue that if you put your money in an interest-bearing account then your money is making money. This may appear to be true on the surface but what is actually happening is the money you placed in the financial institutions is being used by that institution to extend loans to other individuals and companies to purchase homes, expand services, start businesses and initiate commerce. Based upon these "ideas in action" the banks charge interest rates to those borrowers and from those returns they pay the "savers" a small percentage of their profits. As long as the bank is making money then you will also make some money but it's not because your money is actually sitting someplace safe. Make no doubt about it; your money is being used to put someone else's ideas into action. All is well and good as long as the economy is growing but as soon as the economy begins to retract, you better believe those returns you were getting are going to decrease if not disappear all together.

This may seem like a small matter, but the point is to realize that there ultimately is no "safe place" for your money. All types of accounts have some degree of risk. Even if a financial institution says an account is "guaranteed or no risk" there are limits to the amount and you must ensure the accounts are structured properly. It may take an extreme act of the bank going bankrupt but as we've seen over the past few years this isn't always as rare of an event as many may think. Banks can and do sometimes default. Even if the government steps in, you need to understand they certainly do not have a bottomless pit of money to just distribute to everyone. Smart investors understand that you don't get something for nothing. It is by putting your money into action that it gains power to create additional income but understand that every investment opportunity, no matter how conservative, has some degree of risk.

The question for you as an investor is, "how much risk are you comfortable with"? Another way to ask this question is, "in what type of companies can I put my money into action that I believe will prove to be profitable"? Obviously, there are a lot of companies that can achieve that goal. Some will do it more "safely" while others may appear more "unstable" but may likewise produce greater returns. It is pretty safe to say that McDonald's is not going anywhere anytime soon. Of course, many other investors know this as well so investing in this company may provide you some steady returns over a long period of time but likewise may not make you rich. Wouldn't you have liked to invest in Microsoft back in the 70's when it was first coming about? I actually have an uncle who went to Harvard at the same time as Bill Gates. According to him he says he actually remembers Bill Gates going around asking for investors. It may sound like a "no brainer" now to invest in his company but thirty something years ago it probably wasn't so simple. Technology has evolved and made certain products instrumental to our everyday lives but back then computers were bulky and expensive and very few could imagine that one day everyone would want, much less need, one in their homes. These people, like Henry Ford, had the vision to see how the world could benefit from a product and be changed forever.

The important keys to remember here is that money doesn't make money, it is putting ideas into action, which often requires money that creates business and thus profits. You may have creative ideas of your own that you want to put your money behind or you may have family, friends or complete strangers that may approach you with ideas with the opportunity to make money. Some opportunities may seem too good to be true while others may seem highly improbable. Either may be the once in a lifetime opportunity to change your life forever. You will have to carefully examine the details, ask a lot of questions and try to peer into the future to try to determine if a vision may one day come into fruition. It will certainly take action on someone's part to determine if that dream really comes true.

Financial Tip: *I will put my money into ideas that make sense and resonate with me. I will not be foolhardy by chasing profits that may be short-lived.*

Coach says...

I spent some time in the Navy as a student pilot. As part of that training, it is important for you to know how to be a good swimmer. We would have to practice swimming a mile with a flight suit on. They would also use a simulator to dunk you into a pool to teach you how to escape from a plane that just struck water and is sinking. One of the first things they teach you is to not panic when under stress and of course nothing stresses you more than the feeling that you can't breathe. However, remaining calm is exactly what you must do to increase your chances of survival. If you already have a short supply of oxygen, then panicking is only going to cause you to burn up that oxygen more quickly therefore lessening your amount of time to remedy the situation.

In our daily routines, life will also present situations that may cause us to naturally want to respond under stressed conditions. In order to best make the "right" choices to create the best outcome you must remain calm, examine the situation to the best of your ability with the information available and the allotted time you have to decide, and act accordingly as opposed to "reacting" under duress.

We may not always get what we want from an experience but sometimes the lesser of two evils or the best option out of many bad options may still mean the difference between a "bump in the road" and complete catastrophe. It is our inability to remain calm when acting that causes us to often make bad situations worse. We must also understand that life waits for no one. There are those that get so overwhelmed with trying to make the "right" decision that they fail to make any decision at all and by the time they get ready to decide, a decision has already been made for them. Because we live in a world where one person's decision may affect others, your inability to decide doesn't mean that the rest of the world has stopped acting. Hindsight is always 20/20 but you will not always have the luxury of time to decide.

I recall one particular story of a Naval Captain of a ship that shot down a commercial aircraft killing all the people on board. I'm sure this is a decision he will always regret. I don't know the details of the scenario but apparently, they had sent radio messages to the aircraft but failed to get a response. The plane was getting nearer with each passing moment. The captain had to decide if this plane was threatening or not. Given the little bit of information he had, he chose to fire upon the plane. This is an extreme example, one that many of us hope to never have to be in but imagine if he decided to not protect his ship and crew. If that plane had been antagonistic, it could've sunk the entire ship killing everyone onboard; the ship held many more people than the plane did. It is unfortunate because people died either way but given the situation, he made the best decision he could. If he were faced with the same predicament, he would probably make the same choice. Fortunately, most business decisions are not quite that grave. So, if you never want to be in a situation to have to make that sort of life or death decision then you're probably not cut out to be a Naval Captain. Likewise, if you are unable to make business decisions that sometimes fail then you are also not cut out to be a business owner.

Regardless, if you are a business owner or not even as an employee you will have to learn to be decisive and know how and when to act. As the saying goes, "Scared money doesn't make money." Taking action is a crucial quality of leadership and success. You must be able to understand and define your intention, communicate those goals to others and lead by setting the example with clear action. In the famous words of Franklin D. Roosevelt, "There is nothing to fear but fear itself."

Success Skill: *I understand that I may not always make the best decision with the information available at hand but to be a creator, I must take control and act when it matters!*

"Knowing is not enough; we must apply. Willing is not enough; we must do!"

Johann Wolfgang van Goethe

THE PRINCIPLE OF ENERGY

*"And what is a man without **energy**? Nothing... nothing at all!"*

Mark Twain

Advisor says...

Every company knows the importance of its sales force. That's why if a business ever starts to struggle, the last people often laid off will be the sales team. The sales people are typically the only employees actually bringing money in through the front doors. Without paying customers, you don't have a business. People who have worked in sales know the best sales people are the ones who have conviction in their product and present it with high energy. This doesn't mean you have to be bouncing off the walls like a hyper child, but you do have to be able to identify the temperament of your client and approach them with the appropriate degree of enthusiasm that they will appreciate.

This should also be your approach towards your financial and investment decisions. If you approach all decisions related to money as if you are giving away a kidney, you would never enjoy the prosperity that may come from it. Money should be used and circulated and not hoarded like it is your lifeline. I'm not suggesting you spend like there's no tomorrow, although the truth is there may not be a tomorrow for you, I'm simply stating that you have to have the right attitude and energy towards positive usage of your finances. If you know that you do not possess the time and the right temperament towards investment decisions, then it may serve you better to hire a professional to manage them for you.

Most investment firms offer discretionary accounts. These are investment accounts where a professional will tailor an investment strategy that corresponds with your risk tolerance and goals and then they'll actually select the funds for you and manage them accordingly. You typically have to have a certain amount of money for these accounts and you should be aware of what trading fees they will charge you. Churning is a term where an investor makes unnecessary changes to your portfolio with the sole purpose of creating commissions for themselves. It is unethical and heavily guarded against by the SEC or FINRA but that doesn't mean that every advisor abides by the rules or won't attempt to justify why they made these changes to your portfolio.

These are just a couple potential cons of this type of account, but it does have quite a few pros as well. These advisors are professionals who will typically be aware of market trends and company profile changes long before the average person.

They spend their days monitoring the promising companies and mutual funds and they will generally know the best holding period to help you achieve your financial goals. Most importantly, these professionals will tend to be more level headed, less emotional and realistic when it comes to performance. They should accordingly approach your portfolio with a greater degree of optimism and enthusiasm because the investment strategy makes good sense as opposed to following the emotional roller coaster of bull and bear markets.

Financial Tip: *I understand that money or ideas in action possess true power and value. I will energize my dollars through smart investing.*

Yogi says...

Again, these principles are delicately being laid out for you to establish a most effective approach in manifesting prosperity. Followed closely, they will help to ensure you are in the best frame of being, consciousness and mindset to create results. As you begin taking action to manifest your goals, it is important that you do so with the right kind of energy. Your energy is generally a reflection of your attitude. So, the first thing to do is ensure you have the right attitude. The "right" attitude is one that influences those around you in such a way that they work in harmony with you to help achieve goals. So, ask yourself, "Do people generally respond better to positive and upbeat energy or negative and degrading energy"? The answer hopefully should be obvious.

Everything is energy in motion. We, as creators, are no different. We must simply know how to generate and bring forth the right kind of energy. Many studies have shown that successful people tend to be optimistic in nature. So, no matter what may go wrong, you have to be able to see the silver lining, keep a positive attitude and express good energy towards others. If you are not already this type of person, then it will take considerable time and effort to nurture these qualities, but you can do it with the right determination. This will begin with a clear presence of mind and then reprogramming yourself to not get consumed with what goes wrong. Immediately upon hearing bad news, you should remain quiet for a moment to try to get the full story. Once you feel you have all the complete information, although this may not always be apparent, you have to figure out how to transform what may appear to be negative into something that you can channel into something more positive.

If it is something like the passing of a loved one, friend or coworker, there's really not a good way to tell someone that a person has died. The best you can do is try to be empathetic and be supportive immediately. Let that person know that they are not alone, and you are there for them should they need you. It is best not to try to spin this sort of information into something positive. Everyone will grieve differently. You must give people the space they need to do so in their own way. Once you feel that this sort of ordeal has been addressed properly, you may then begin to try to find ways to be proactive. An outing, mural, cards, flowers and so forth may be appropriate signs of appreciation and recognition at the right time. However, at some point in time a healthy healing process will require a change in "energy" from sorrow to celebration for a person's life. Hence, this brings us to two important aspects of energy. They are optimism and service.

First, let's talk about service. We often hear catch phrases like "change the world" but if you really think about it it's impossible to change the world. The world is nothing more than a collective reflection of the characteristics of individuals. We all know it is impossible to change another person hence it is equally impossible to change the world, which again is nothing more than billions of individuals. If you can't change one, then you certainly can't change billions. Sure, we can try to create laws and institutions to try to control or modify behaviors, but you are not really changing people therefore you are not changing the world. The world is full of prisons with convicts who've committed every crime imaginable.

This isn't meant to be discouraging but if we can't change people or the world what can we do? The best thing we, as individuals, can do is to try to inspire people to want to change themselves! And what is the best way to get people to want to change themselves? By being the example and serving others by trying to fill a void or need they may have. The truth is we, as souls, are not lacking anything. It is only through desire that we imagine we need something outside of ourselves but until each individual comes to that realization on their own, we can help one another by serving one another. Everyone needs love. Everyone needs encouragement, support, understanding, food, clothing, shelter and so forth. If you truly want to make an impact upon those around you and the world at large for the better, then begin to think of yourself as a giver and provider.

To make your giving as magnificent as possible, you should do so enthusiastically and optimistically. This sort of energy is contagious and transfers good cheer that multiplies as it is exchanged. When you bring a smile to someone's face, it helps to put them in a better mood, and they are much more likely to forward that good vibration to others they encounter. Even if someone doesn't seem that receptive, your good cheer will help to minimize whatever ill mood that person may be going through at the time. Positive energy cannot help but have an impact on another for the better.

When it comes to selling an idea or trying to persuade others, the most effective people will be the ones who do so with uplifting energy. Every great salesperson knows the truth of this statement. People don't always buy because of a product; they buy because of the person. If someone seems to really be excited about an item, then others want to buy that person's "enthusiasm" as well. They want to see what all the excitement is for themselves. I once went to a restaurant and asked the waiter for his recommendation. He began to enthusiastically tell me about his favorite item on the menu. I could his eyes glistening and his mouth watering as if he were about to actually take a bite. It just so happens that I didn't take his recommendation. It wasn't because of his presentation though, it was because of my particular diet but had it not been for that conflict I would have certainly tried it. Nonetheless, we did spark up good conversation and I had a pleasant dining experience simply because his excitement transferred to me and there wasn't much else he could have done wrong at that point. He also earned himself a nice tip for his work. That is the power of optimistic service!

Spiritual Practice: *My goal is to serve others in the most enjoyable way possible. By uplifting others, I help to uplift myself.*

Coach says...

Motivation takes the form of expressed energy as well. Negative motivation and positive motivation are the two ends of the spectrum as displays of intended energy. The military long known for its reputation of molding soldiers often used negative motivation to "whip" cadets into shape. However, they are now coming to better understand the usage of positive energy and motivation. While negative motivation may still have its place, the military is recognizing that it tends to be short lived while positive motivation boosts morale and lasts much longer with the troops. Motivation is a direct reflection of positive and negative energy being used to influence others.

Attitude and energy are perhaps the two most essential qualities in not only leadership but in success. One of my first most valuable lessons happened in boot camp. I was a young 17 years old sailor appointed as Master at Arms for our company. The Master at Arms is basically the second person in charge of managing the daily routines and functions of the recruits. We had just returned to our barracks from dinner for the evening when our company commander shouted out "Warnick!!" and

I went running into his office and snapped to attention. He began to question me as to why his trash had not been taken out. I insisted that I had told one of the fellow Seaman in the company to take it out and my commander then told me to drop and do pushups. At the time I couldn't understand why he was punishing me for someone else's failure to do their job. He then explained to me that I could delegate responsibility to others, but I couldn't delegate accountability. Simply telling someone else to do something wasn't enough. I had to ensure that they did it because ultimately, I was going to be the one accountable.

That lesson stuck with me over the years. It was an attempt to instill the right attitude of leadership in me. Another lesson would come many years later when I was in the NROTC unit in preparation for becoming an Officer. We were setting up for a visit from an Admiral, so everyone was on deck to make sure everything was prepared properly. We were a little behind on schedule so suddenly our base XO, executive officer, began lifting chairs to place them for the audience. Up to this point in my five-year career, I had never seen a high-ranking officer lift a finger to do this sort of menial manual labor. So, several of us cadets told him we would take care of the chairs. He looked at us rather silly and said he could move a few chairs. In that moment he gained the respect of all the cadets present. He showed us by example that he wasn't too good to do manual labor and something as minor as moving chairs wasn't beneath him at this stage in his military career. From that point forward, we would've gone out of our ways to be there for him in anyway he may have requested. He earned that respect because he didn't just preach one thing and practice another rather, he led by example and proved he wouldn't ask something of us that he wasn't willing to do himself.

These are just a couple of small examples of how the right attitude and positive energy affects those around you. As another quick example, we once had a Chief stationed at a base in Albany, Georgia. Everyday we would see this Chief passing by, and we would ask him how his day was and no matter what he would respond, "It's a super fantastic day!" This became the norm so we would expect this answer and sure enough he would never disappoint. Now obviously, I don't truly believe every day could've really been "super fantastic" but whether it truly was or not it surely brought a smile to our faces. This does, however, stress an important point. The words we express have a twofold effect. Not only do they transfer a certain impression and energy to others, but they help to create and manifest our own experience. If you say it enough in one day that you are having a "super fantastic" day, I would dare to say that your day might in fact turn out to be just that. This may not prove to be a 100% rule but if we were to keep a record I would certainly not be surprised if in fact that person's perception is that they indeed did have a great day. Remember it's all relative. Your words are powerful and do possess energy that impacts everyone around you.

Many years later, I actually made an attempt to put my former Chief's positive attitude into practice. I was teaching seventh grade math and science. I probably don't have to tell you that most thirteen-year-olds aren't exactly excited about math. So, in an effort to try and counter that attitude I came up with a quote at the beginning of each class to tell the students why today was a good day to learn math. I started out saying "everyday was a good day to learn math." Then it became silly stuff like "the Chicago Bulls won last night therefore it's a good day to learn math" or "it's going to be a sunny 80 degrees outside therefore it's a good day to learn math." Initially, I got a lot of rolled eyes, moans and groans, jeers and heckles but once I showed them that I was going to consistently put a quote up at the beginning of the class they began to get into it. In fact, I actually created a monster. If I tried to begin class and had forgotten to write something on the board, they would quickly remind me "Mr. Warnick, you forgot to write up a reason to learn math today!" So, they began to hold me accountable and I likewise took enjoyment in the fact that something that simple would resonate with them to get some sort of positive energy from math class.

My middle school teaching career would prove to be short-lived. We only got paid once a month and after taxes the pay didn't amount to much. I enjoyed the students but had a difficult time with the administration. From the beginning of the school year, the principal focused on nothing but end-of-grade test scores. The principal all the way down to the lower staff got bonuses if the students achieved certain scores. I can understand the motivation of that but in my humble opinion it took away from actual learning. I tried to connect with my students on their level, bring some fun, energy and excitement to the class but my principal disagreed with my approach.

I would create games and competition through team efforts to learn problems, which would cause the class to sometimes get rowdy. I felt it was acceptable as long as everyone was involved. My principal continuously warned me that she didn't think my class would benefit from that strategy and their end-of-grade test results would suffer. My principal wanted me to run my class like boot camp, which is why I guess she hired me, but I refused to teach that way. Long story short, my class had the highest growth in their test scores compared to their peers at the end of the year. I respect all teachers but feel it is sad that our education system approaches learning like a business. It punishes good, creative teachers and attempts to mold a cookie cutter approach that lacks positive attitude and uplifting energy.

Success Skill: *The energy I express is the energy I get in return. Positive, enthusiastic and optimistic energy produce better results than negative, degrading and pessimistic energy.*

*"**Energy** and persistence alter all things."*
Benjamin Franklin

THE PRINCIPLE OF NON-JUDGMENT

"Judgments prevent us from seeing the good that lies beyond appearances."

Wayne Dyer

Yogi says...

As we advance through the stages of these ten principles and begin interacting with our environments with the intention of producing certain results, we must incorporate a practice of non-judgment. Our actions and energy are going to begin producing all sorts of experiences and results that may appear to come to us or that we "attracted" but in truth they are merely a direct result of what we created. This difference in perspective is crucial. If you merely believe that you attracted something to you from elsewhere then you may not want to accept responsibility for that experience but if you recognize that all experiences are simply the result of what you **created** then you empower yourself to know that you can change any experience by creating a new one!

Another important aspect of non-judgment is humility. We must all acknowledge that we are not creations of our own doing. No one has come to this earth without parents. Even Jesus Christ, who you may believe was immaculately conceived, humbly acknowledged he was about his Father's work. He only sought to serve what he believed to be the Creator's will. Even though he had weak moments, felt betrayed and sometimes thought the burden was too heavy, he persevered because he felt he had a calling larger than his own desires. If you want to live like Christ, then the way to live is unselfishly for others without judgment of the experiences that may come our way. Similarly, we must all recognize that we are only pieces of a much larger puzzle. To achieve your greatest potential that may "change the world," you must see beyond your own personal attainments. If you judge every encounter as good or bad or whether or not it serves you then you are missing out on potential opportunities to help you grow as an individual and to serve a greater good.

The reason why most of us judge experiences is because we either have an expectation of how things are supposed to work or a desire to be in a certain place. If something doesn't match our expectation, then we tend to judge it negatively. We like to categorize things as a "success" when it is a goal that we accomplished, and it matches our expectation and equally judge things as "failures" when we don't reach a goal or something doesn't meet our expectations. But what if we let go of expectations all together? What if we didn't judge each experience? What if we set goals but were able to accept every outcome in advance and told ourselves every outcome was a blessing? This may sound like a quantum leap for many but the better you are able to live this way, the freer you become and the more satisfied with life you will be.

The problem for most people who lack prosperity is that they envision a better life when they are able to attain greater wealth. While it is true that having financial resources affords you a lifestyle with greater choices than without money, it isn't true that this automatically equates to happiness. Happiness is what we are truly seeking. Even those who already possess considerable wealth realize that happiness is fleeting. As long as you attach your happiness to material objects then you will never experience real happiness. Happiness is not a reflection of your accumulation of possessions. It is an expression of your state of being. Even a homeless person can be happy when they realize that it comes from within. When we discover proper understanding of ourselves, we then realize that we are in control of our happiness, and lack thereof, by our internal dialogue. For most of us, our happiness is directly influenced by our state of mind. When you are able to develop and control a state of mind without judgment and receive every experience as a blessing then you will have mastered peace and happiness.

No experience is inherently good or bad; not even death. It is only our judgment about that experience that we tell ourselves if it was good or bad. Learn to accept every experience as a blessing. Either it assists in moving you in the direction closer to the life you have chosen, or it moves you in another direction. However, that new direction doesn't mean you've moved backwards for it is actually impossible to go backwards. You can never be the person you were yesterday. Each day you live and gain new experiences and memories means you've changed eternally as a person. Simply see any changes in direction as part of a process to make your wiser and more complete.

Rudyard Kipling in his poem "If" calls triumph and disaster both imposters. The reason is because they are both not real. In fact, every experience is temporary and thus contains no permanency. Anything that is not permanent is therefore a transitory illusion. The only thing guaranteed in life is death but even this only means death of your physical form. You as a soul will live on. It is through becoming "in tune" with your eternal soul consciousness that you become master of your fate. When you understand that every experience contains elements of failure and success then you won't become victim to the changing tides of nature. Every person who may be deemed a "success" knows they went through, most likely, many more "failures" on the road to reaching their goals.

Truth be told, they would have never achieved that success had it not been for those failures. You should think of failures as precursors or messengers foretelling you of your impending success. This way you can take some solace in knowing that success is on its way! Every failure is like finding your way through a maze. If you come to a dead end, rather than become frustrated, you should take delight that you've eliminated one more possible path that didn't bring you to your desired destination. The more "wrong" paths you check off your list, the closer you are to finding the correct path. They say Benjamin Franklin failed to successfully create a workable light bulb many times over. Another way to look at it is that he repeatedly succeeded in making a non-workable light bulb. Each rough draft helped move him closer his goal. Even if he had gone to his grave trying, his work would have been a roadmap for others to follow, which would have helped someone to finally succeed. When your "purpose" is larger than yourself and you refrain from selfish judgment then you open up the floodgates of opportunity for prosperity for you and others.

Spiritual Practice: *I will practice even-mindedness under all extreme circumstances. Clarity of mind will help me to come to the best solutions.*

Advisor says...

Late February to early March of 2009 proved to be the low point of the financial markets in the most recent recession. Banks were failing, foreclosures were at an all time high, unemployment was dreadful, the U.S. was at war and anxieties were at their worse. Yet those who were able to approach their financial decisions without judgment saw a once in a lifetime opportunity to capitalize on a great climate for investing. Every investor understands the simple notion of "buy low and sell high." This strategy sounds easy enough but what comes along with that is a lot of emotional fear and paranoia. Prices being low means people's confidence is also low therefore the last thing you want to do is to take risk. However, when people's confidence is high, people want to take chances, but this typically means they are buying in a market that is high as well.

The problem is that we are making judgments about circumstances and these judgments influence our emotions and thus our decision-making. The only emotion I can say may be worthwhile when it comes to investing is passion for what you're investing in. Even this emotion is limiting because there are a lot of great companies to invest in that will produce returns that you may not have a passion for. The vice versa is true as well; just because you have a passion for something doesn't mean the business will thrive. The only reason I say passion can be helpful in terms of investing is that it will most likely help to make it fun and keep you interested. When you have a passion for something you are more prone to look up information on the company, research reports, follow it on the news and read articles. Other than that, you should approach your investment decisions without emotional judgment and utilize the best available information, the advice of a professional and common sense.

I must admit that at the low of the market in 2009, I even began second-guessing my investment advice. After continuing to see the downward trend, I started thinking maybe this time is different. Maybe the sky really is falling. Perhaps we should all take cover. If you watch the news long enough, you'll start to believe all the hysteria. But then I had to reassess the situation and remind myself of a few things. First, the media is NOT objective. They used to do a better job with being impartial in the news, many decades ago, but now it is so clouded with hype and personal opinion. The reason is that the huge news outlets are financed by television networks that have an agenda of getting the most viewers possible so they can sell advertising to clients in the form of commercials. Through extensive studies and experience, stations realize that controversy, sex and catchy sound bites are what bring in the viewers.

The truth is the stock markets and financial matters tend to be pretty boring stuff. So, to increase ratings, the media will often over exaggerate the market swings and what they mean. Of course, people's perceptions about the market then influence people's actions and the market tends to overshoot on the highs and lows based upon public opinion. I had to remind myself that I had a long-term investment strategy and I was nowhere near ready to pull money out of my investments. So why am I ready to react to swings that will most likely happen several more times before I actually reach retirement? The market goes through these sorts of cycles roughly every 6 to 8 years. So, I had to calm my emotional judgments about the markets, economy and so forth and stick with a logical approach. This strategy proved to be correct now that the markets are back to normal. In fact, the smartest thing to have done in hindsight would've been to buy up more shares of good companies and mutual funds when they were "on sale" at a low price. If in fact, the sky really had fallen then the world would have had much bigger problems than the dollars I might've lost in investments. Many people feel the world economy may be heading for that ill fate but if that is ever the case then governments will have to create a new system for people to survive. No one wants chaos and anarchy.

Non-judgment should be our approach in life, everyday matters and creating prosperity. As we tread our unique paths, it behooves us to practice non-judgment about each and every event. Give things time to pan out. Gather the best information available, seek a second opinion if necessary and try to make logical choices based on facts and not just emotion. The less we judge, the clearer our thinking and the better decisions we can make towards achieving our goals.

Financial Tip: *Money has no emotion or judgment. It's true value only lies in the ideas and beliefs of the masses. I will use these facts to my advantage in approaching financial matters.*

Coach says...

When we are referring to judgments it is important to stress that we are referring to emotional conclusions drawn from personal opinion and not discriminative reasoning. The military along with doctors, policemen, fire fighters and so forth are some of the few professions that may deal with life and death situations frequently. Most of us in our careers don't deal with life threatening situations in our career choices or managing our businesses.

However, when one of these professionals is making decisions they are not doing so from emotional judgment. They are doing so from rational reasoning. The military along with these other professions are trained on how to stay calm, keep their heads and assess situations quickly and decide how to respond. They run drills often to simulate stressing situations so that the individual is familiar with high-pressure scenarios so hopefully their training kicks in when faced with a real-life version.

I'm not suggesting that they ever become perfect at this but if you look at the track records you will see that they are in large part successful. There may be occasional incidences where a soldier may have allowed his or her emotional judgment to shoot and kill someone not from their training but from a moment of emotional misjudgment. Likewise, we often hear stories of police officer's that may have overreacted to a suspect not based upon a real and actual threat but based upon a stereotype such as racial profiling. Again, going back to the media, they unfortunately will talk about these incidences disproportionately because it is controversial and will draw in greater ratings. They may try to justify their coverage by stating they're merely keeping these institutions accountable, but they can't dispute that they also get the benefit of ratings and thus greater sponsorship.

The key point here is if the military and other professionals can be trained to remain calm, think clearly and make appropriate decisions based on actual data then you can also train yourself to remove emotional judgment from the equation. This will allow you to accept and appreciate the diverse dynamics of life and prosperous living. I remember the magician Criss Angel being interviewed about his success and how he's handled it. He stated that while he appreciates it, it isn't quite what a lot of people imagine. He may have cars, houses and fame but doesn't often have the time to enjoy it. One of his mentors told him it's not getting to the destination but rather enjoying the journey. He said he understands that advice much better now. We often become so consumed with achieving a goal that we fail to enjoy the scenery of getting there. Some of the best times will be when we recall having close friends and family near, having to sleep on the floor, driving an old beat up car or whatever "less than desirable" roads we have to trudge.

If we are constantly judging moments, then we will fail to see the instrumental parts that may unfold. It's like going to see an orchestra and listening only for the wrong or misplayed notes. If you only critique the mishaps in life, then you fail to appreciate the full symphony. Life is like a beautiful soundtrack. There will be high notes and low notes, intensity and serenity, up tempos and down tempos, theatrics and comedy, romance and suspense, losing and winning but you must try not to judge every play by play and embrace it all. In the words of Ferris Bueller, **"Life moves pretty fast. If you don't stop and look around once in a while, you could miss it."**

Success Skill: *Nothing is inherently good or bad. It is only my judgment about it. To change an experience, I must not judge it and accept that they are all opportunities for me to grow.*

"As you inquire into issues and turn judgments around, you come to see that every perceived problem appearing "out there" is really nothing more than a misperception within your own thinking."

Byron Katie

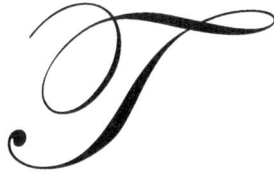

THE PRINCIPLE OF NON-ATTACHMENT

"The awakened sages call a person wise when all his undertakings are free from anxiety about results."

Krishna

Advisor says...

When approaching your investment or financial choices you must likewise go into them with a certain degree of non-attachment. If you cannot let go of money, then you don't need to be investing. If you compulsively monitor your dollars you will either drive yourself crazy or lose a lot of money from excessive trading. This is why your investment decisions must be goal driven and not profit driven! Markets can change drastically in little to no time. If you are holding on to an investment because you simply think it's going to keep rising, then you are losing sight of your goal. Likewise, if you are withdrawing or selling shares because the market is low, even though you may not need the money, then you will never make money.

No matter how savvy of an investor you are, no one can say they've mastered timing the market. There are just too many potential factors and variables that can impact changes. However, there are trends. The market over a 10-year period typically averages 8 to 10% returns. Most advisors will generally lower the expectation by quoting lower numbers so that if you get a higher return then they've exceeded your expectation. So, the goal for the average investor is to use the statistics to your advantage. If you stay focused on your goal and therefore know your necessary holding periods, then you should achieve those goals with the right investment strategy. There is no guarantee that you will win on every investment but if you're properly diversified then you should win on more opportunities than you lost and thus you will have an overall gain.

This, however, requires you to be emotionally non-attached. You must use logic when it comes to wise decision making. If you are consumed with the money you "left on the table" because you followed your investment strategy and reallocated your assets at the planned period, then you are losing sight of your accomplishment. Hindsight is always 20/20 when you know what the markets already did but what if your suspicion was that the market was going to continue climbing but instead it suddenly plunges? Most recessions will typically take 2 to 3 years to make up for the losses and you may not have that time to recoup that money. This is why it is imperative to develop a long and short-term investment strategy, review it at pre-planned intervals, and stick to the game plan. You should only changes strategies "mid stream" if you realize that you are clearly in a portfolio that is way out of whack for your risk tolerance or if some significant life event takes place like a new baby, death, change of career or income, divorce, change in health, bankruptcy or unemployment and so forth. The market is generally driven by fear and greed. You don't want to let either of these clouded emotions dictate your investment selections.

Financial Tip: *I will not allow fear and greed to control my financial decisions. Proper planning and logic are superior to emotional attachment.*

Coach says...

The success skill most closely related to non-attachment would have to be adaptability or flexibility.

The reality of life is that things don't always go as planned so the way to rise above these situations is to be able to see a new avenue and adapt quickly. This doesn't mean you have to be "flighty" and go "every which way" the wind blows. Once you've taken considerable time to set your goals then you shouldn't let small matters dissuade you. However, you must also recognize there is more than one way to "skin a cat" as they say. As long as you reach your goal without having to sell your soul, does it matter which path gets you there? Sometimes we prevent ourselves from reaching goals because we refuse to take another path that life seems to be pointing us in.

Adaptability is a useful quality that the military tries to instill in its officers. If you have a certain plan of attack that is failing then you must be able to weigh options and quickly figure out if there is another way to accomplish the mission without sacrificing unnecessary personnel, resources or equipment. Life and business are often a "push-pull" relationship. If you remain rigid unable to bend or compromise, then forces beyond your control may snap your progress due to stubbornness. Practicing resolve doesn't mean that you become totally unyielding. Being flexible and able to adapt to new information as it presents itself is a vital quality to success and prosperity.

The road to success can often produce "casualties of war." Anything worth attaining doesn't always come easily. I've had moments in life where I've tried to make situations work against all odds. On one hand you can say struggling in such circumstances can make you stronger and there is no denying that. On the other hand, some of my greatest "successes" only came after I was able to accept some "failures." Many travels in life may be individually unique and yet still hold universal truths. If it is only your pride that is making you "stay the course" then you may continue to take crushing blows until you are able to swallow that pride. I challenge you to find an example of someone that remained "on top of the world" without having their ego checked. Those whose pride causes them to believe they are invincible generally get "knocked down" a peg or two by their own karma.

I won't bother trying to name famous people but we all can think of a celebrity or two who seemed to let their heads get too big. If they learn some humility then they may recover quickly but if they insist on trying to be "larger than life," they may lose everything they've worked hard for simply from an inability to let go of their pride. We all have different roles to play in life but that doesn't mean because one person's role may be more "front and center" that they are somehow worthier than another. The quarterback of a football team may draw most of the attention, but I have yet to see a quarterback win a football game without ten other players on the field. Success and prosperity are often the result of team efforts.

Success Skill: *I will lead by example. Prosperity should be shared amongst everyone and not just myself.*

Yogi says...

It is important to recognize that what we "experience" is relative, and our control stops once we have acted. Of course, we can choose to continue to react depending upon our experiences but even in reacting, we have no control over what comes next. This detail or nuance is important to recognize! Most of us go crazy attempting to control outcomes when the truth is once we have done our part to the best of our ability, our control stops there. Yet most of us don't "act" with the satisfaction that we have done our part. We often make the mistake of selfishly seeking return. If we do a favor for a friend, then we expect a favor to be returned to us. If we do something charitable for another then we expect gratitude in return. It is these unfulfilled expectations and desires that cause most personal anguish. When we get what we want, we are happy. When we don't get what we want, we tend to be unhappy. It is too much emotional attachment to desires and expectations that prevents us from experiencing our greatest prosperity. When you detach from objects and allow them to flow fluidly through you, you then become a conduit or medium for all sorts of blessings, opportunities and experiences. I reiterate; we must redefine our understanding of prosperity. It is not about how much wealth we hoard but more about our quality of life and our contentment with ourselves.

If you want to be "master of your fate and captain of your soul" then you must not be the slave to material possessions. It is our attachment that gives objects power over us and we behave like misers instead of kings and queens. Show me a person that is quick to anger, and I'll show you someone who isn't able to accept not always getting his or her way. To control frustration, you must alter your internal dialogue and to be completely free you must embody non-attachment.

The Native Americans are great examples of a culture that understood non-attachment. They didn't consider themselves to own property or earthly objects. The considered themselves to merely be temporary caretakers of their homes, livestock, vegetation and so forth. They respected the planet and lived in harmony with the transient nature of things. Society has obviously evolved drastically but these ancient understandings remain true to this day. To truly be fulfilled and content you should cherish and honor your possessions without being attached to them. Recognize that all things come and go, and you will be able to enjoy them much more while they last. Approach life with this attitude and it will ensure that you always have an abundance that exceeds your needs.

Life is designed to help you become the best person you can be. People who are consumed with holding on to everything are forced to repeat experiences over and over again. The truth is sometimes we don't know what is best for us. When we try to force issues, we are potentially blocking greater blessings that are coming to us. Allow things to come and go and you open up the world of opportunities. The universe moves in cycles. The planets, solar systems and galaxies all rotate. Things come and go. Daytime is followed by nighttime. The ocean, sounds and light all travel in waves with peaks and valleys, crests and troughs. Imagine if you tried to hold on to the greatest moment of your life forever. It would lose its "greatness" because you would have nothing else to compare it with. You would also prevent yourself from experiencing **different** moments that may prove to be equally as great, if not greater!

Spiritual Practice: *I accept that all things change. Through non-attachment, I open myself up to infinite possibilities.*

"Misery is nothing but the shadow of attachment and hence all stagnancy. The attached person becomes a stagnant pool — sooner or later he will stink! He flows no more…"

Osho

129

THE PRINCIPLE OF RECIPROCITY

"If your only goal is to become rich, you will never achieve it."

John D. Rockefeller

Coach says...

Reciprocity is the secret to success! I've tried to provide examples of people who've practiced what they've preached, led by example and treated others the way they wanted to be treated. All good leaders look out for their troops whether this may literally be soldiers, employees, family, children or whomever. The goal to strive for is that there is no difference in your words and your actions. When your thoughts, words and actions all coincide you become a powerful force to be reckoned with. Your resolve and determination will either align supporters with you or remove obstacles in your way. The key is to not try and dominate others rather do things with others in mind and thus you ensure that their reactions to you never become a hindrance to your goals. This is reciprocity in practice.

The military is the epitome of teamwork at its finest. The goals and mission take precedence over any one individual. The whole of the team unit is what is most important. No system is perfect, but the military comes closest to putting aside differences in race, religion, gender and as of late sexual preference. It is the experimental melting pot. What is most important is our intention, how we treat others and a team mentality. The energy we emit typically is reciprocated back to us. If you seek to be successful, then you should help others to be successful in their endeavors. You can do this by sharing your knowledge with others, serving as a mentor, instructor or personal coach. Make it part of who you are to provide guidance to those who need it and you will find those in a position to help you willing to assist you as well.

One lesson I learned, and we continuously attempted to incorporate in military life, was the attitude that you should try to know your boss' job. If your supervisor ever separated, retired, got promoted or worse killed in action, each subordinate's duty was to be able to try to fill that person's shoes in a moment's notice. This ensured continuity and the smoothest transition possible. Your goal should be that when your boss changes position that you are the first person that comes to mind for his or her replacement. Likewise, good managers and leaders understand that they should reciprocate this ideal by trying to groom their personnel to do their job.

I know this isn't always the world we live in, particularly in the civilian world of business, because people often feel threatened or need to "protect" their job by remaining valuable to the company. This idea that you can be "irreplaceable" to a company not only hurts the company but ultimately limits you as well. If a company needs you to fulfill one job duty and you offer no other talents, then how do you ever grow or get promoted? Likewise, if the day comes where they can find someone to do your job for a lower salary then why would they keep you?

Most people, unfortunately, approach important career and business decisions from a base of fear but that will stifle you from reaching your greatest potential. You should always attempt to treat others the way you would like to be treated. If you know you would like the opportunity to be recognized and appreciated for you contributions, then you should try to recognize and appreciate others mutually. Help others to maximize their potential and you will always find opportunities for you to accomplish the same. This is the law of cause and effect, karma or reciprocity. It is all the same. A desire to help others brings help when you need it. A grateful attitude brings gracious blessings to you. Helping others to prosper emblazons you to become a dynamo of prosperity.

Success Skill: *Success cannot be achieved without the help of others along the way. The people I see on the way up will be the same people I see on the way down if I fail to consider all!*

Advisor says...

Because money is merely the creation of man as an idea to represent access to resources, it likewise must abide by this power of reciprocity. The value of money fluctuates depending on many variables with the economy but even in the worst of times there will always be rich people. Likewise, even in these times an ingenious idea still has value. As stated earlier, instead of just seeking how to make profits, you should put your money behind ventures that you truly believe in. Ask yourself, if there were one thing you could change about the world, what would it be? If you can decide what that is then you can do business with companies that share your vision, contribute to non-profits who fulfill that goal and take advantage of the tax write offs or go into business for yourself.

In my line of work as a Financial Advisor when working with a client we will typically follow what's called a Financial Pyramid. This is our way to ensure the client has a strong foundation first and then to build upon that foundation. That foundation starts off with an actual financial plan. That plan is designed to assess the situation, set clear goals, establish priorities, take action by putting the plan into effect and then to periodically review that plan. Once a client has their plan in place, we then step up to the next level, which is to "protect" their assets. It is fairly easy to make plans but as they say, "God is up in heaven laughing at all of our plans" and since things can always go wrong or not according to plan, you must always be in a position to minimize damage. We do this through various instruments such as insurance in the forms of disability, life, long-term care, liability, medical and property and casualty. Then we go to long-range protection such as wills, living wills, principles of attorney and letters of instruction, which is for someone who is not physically able to make decision any longer.

Once we have the proper protections in place we then ascend to the next level on our pyramid, which is to "invest." We advise clients on the most efficient ways to help their money grow. We examine the client's cash flow. This is the comparison of their income to expenses. We ensure they have adequate emergency savings, an up to date budget and their debt is managed effectively. We look at tax strategies to minimize their burdens depending on their income looking at pre-tax spending accounts, health savings accounts, tax advantaged investments, deductions, gifts, credits, exemptions and trusts. We then go to proper retirement planning, funding accounts, contribution amounts, diversification and planned distribution. During this process we include any major purchases, business transfers, college planning for children or grandchildren, home purchases and sales, real estate investments, social security and so forth. Finally, since most clients' knowledge base has long since been exceeded, we work with them to manage these various aspects of their financial health.

What's important to note is that every aspect of what we review with clients is about reciprocity. People aren't really concerned with buying various investment instruments; they are concerned with their quality of life! People can care less about an annuity, mutual fund, stock, insurance, will and so on. They want to know how that vehicle is going to provide for them and their family. People set plans because they have a vision of how they would like to live and intend on how to get there. Most people want a comfortable home to share with their family. They want to be able to entertain guests, relatives and friends. People want to be able to travel to meet new people, indulge in new cultures, try new foods and see new sights. Most people don't want to do these things alone, they want to do them with people they care about.

People don't buy life insurance for themselves they buy it to protect their spouses, parents or children. When you're gone, you're gone but most decent people don't want their families to struggle should they die prematurely. It is already bad enough to lose a loved one, but it is worse to be evicted, foreclosed or have to file bankruptcy over a loss of income on top of that. People establish wills because they care about how their wealth may be used to help family members, non-profit organizations, alma maters, charitable institutions or things they care about. We must remind ourselves that these are the human qualities that are most noble and important. No one wants to live on a deserted island by himself or herself. We are social creatures by nature.

We, unfortunately, sometimes lose sight of what's really important in our lives. Life can be challenging and competitive and we often get caught up in the daily rigmarole of trying to get ahead. We must remind ourselves that we do these things not just for money but because of the things money can provide. Sure houses, cars, boats, clothes, jewelry and so on may bring some degree of pleasure but what good are they without health, love and self-worth? Money can certainly help to alleviate certain ailments of not having it, but it can also foster new issues you may have never realized possible. As the rapper, Notorious B.I.G. stated in his popular song, "More money... more problems."

Even the greatest amounts of money can't fix everything. There are health issues that do not yet have cures and there is nothing more depressing than knowing your money can't fix it or worse you may not be around long enough to even enjoy your money. This is why it is important to take care of your body, mind and spirit now. Enjoy life each and everyday so that as your prosperity increases you get to enjoy it for what its worth and not when its too late. Most importantly, never become consumed with wealth and lose your integrity in lust chase after money. I don't mean to make a mockery out of Bernie Madoff, but he is a prime example of someone that became consumed with the lust for wealth. He thought he had found a way to beat the system. Even though his conscious told him this couldn't go on forever he lacked the self-control to stop himself.

When the money comes in as easily as it was, how do you justify going legit and settling for a fraction of what you can get by breaking the rules? The important key, that all drug dealers equally learn, is that it is all short-lived. The risk isn't worth the reward. Instead of Bernie Madoff enjoying his golden years with his wife and children, he will spend the rest of his days behind bars isolated from whatever wealth he may have accumulated. The law of reciprocity (karma) is unfailing. What you put out comes back to you tenfold! Instead of being selfish and investing all of your energy in accumulating possessions for yourself, use these principles to help make other people's conditions better and the same good energy will come back to you tenfold. This is the essence of prosperity – in body, mind and spirit.

Financial Tip: *Prosperity is not a destination. It is an ongoing experience that I must always nurture through a smart financial platform.*

Yogi says...

What goes around comes around. This is the simplest way of saying what you put out will come back to you. Your life is a reflection of your thoughts and actions. As stressed numerous times already, nothing is yours for the keeping. All things come and go. Rather than try to hold on to possessions and stop the flow of life, try to simply use your intelligence, creativity and will to redirect the flow of blessings to people and ideas that fulfill a greater vision and purpose that benefits others. If you act genuinely and sincerely towards a greater good, then the flow of prosperity will take care of itself. You will never find yourself lacking.

This spiritual power has been expressed in various ways as metaphysical laws. "For every action there is an equal and opposite reaction" is Newton's third law of motion. The law of gravity that every "body of mass" exerts a pull on every other body of mass is also true. These "laws" are merely the observable expressions in grosser form of more subtle spiritual laws. Essentially that which you do unto another shall be done unto you, an eye for an eye or you reap what you sow. These principles are part of the physical universe and cannot be broken.

You may not always be able to witness them in "real" time because there may be a time delay, but they are ultimately unfailing. Rather than try to break these laws, the wise person learns to use them to his or her own benefit.

One way to accomplish this is to make your self of service to others. Anytime you may feel you are lacking something, you should find a way to give that "something" to someone else. If you feel you are lacking in money, try to give something of value to another person in need. If you are completely destitute then you may not be able to give money, but you may be able to fix a person a meal. You may be able to give someone a ride. You may be able to provide shelter. There are numerous ways you can help someone less fortunate. Even if you cannot initially do it from the greatest sincerity, it is still better to do it mechanically than to not do it at all. If you make it a reoccurring routine or habit, then in time it will become more sincere and you will reap greater reward from your actions. This is the subtle law. It doesn't judge it merely operates absolutely.

Even Jesus stated this in Matthew 13:12 ***"For whosoever hath, to him shall be given, and he shall have more abundance: but whosoever hath not, from him shall be taken away even that he hath."*** This is testimony that as you believe in your heart so shall it be. If you think yourself to be poor and act as such then that will be your experience but if you claim your prosperity and share that which you do have then you shall gain more. These are truths that you must trust in. As long as you approach life from a perspective of creativity and service, you will always find yourself in a position to help others and you will be equally compensated. This is law; it is unavoidable. Even if you did charitable work or refused pay for your help, the universe would seek to "repay" you, nonetheless. As you experiment and apply it you will begin to see greater examples and experience it firsthand in your life.

One thing I try to do when I go grocery shopping, pay a bill, repair vehicles, pay business expenses and so forth is to try to bless the money as it exchanges hands, as I write checks or make payments online. I try to remind myself that this money is being used to provide someone a job, help get him or her through school, take care of their families and make their dreams come true. Even big corporations, who may make substantial profits, have to pay their employees, provide benefits and cover their overhead expenses. However, if you think you will feel more gratified by having a clearer outlook on where your money is going then it's your prerogative to only do business with small family owned businesses.

Many customers prefer the intimacy of getting to know the people they do business with personally, so they become loyal to family owned restaurants, auto shops, day cares, food stores, handymen and family practitioners. Ultimately, it doesn't matter who you do business with but more importantly that your own attitude, thoughts and energy are positive as you conduct business and exchange funds. Of course, there are always shady companies out there, but I try to live by the rule "get me once, shame on you; get me twice, shame on me!" You can hope for the most transparent business possible but try to know that as you give, so shall you receive. As long as your intentions are pure then you will always reap the best reward and your prosperity shall multiply.

Spiritual Practice: As I act in the world, I will bless all those I encounter with love and service, trusting in the power of reciprocity.

"It is one of the most beautiful compensations of life that no man can sincerely try to help another without helping himself."

Ralph Waldo Emerson

DON'T QUIT

When things go wrong, as they sometimes will,
When the road you're trudging seems all uphill,
When the funds are low and the debts are high,
And you want to smile, but you have to sigh,
When care is pressing you down a bit,
Rest, if you must, but don't you quit.

Life is queer with its twists and turns,
As every one of us sometimes learns,
And many a failure turns about,
When he might have won had he stuck it out;
Don't give up though the pace seems slow--
You may succeed with another blow.

Often the goal is nearer than,
It seems to a faint and faltering man,
Often the struggler has given up,
When he might have captured the victor's cup,
And he learned too late when the night slipped down,
How close he was to the golden crown.

Success is failure turned inside out--
The silver tint of the clouds of doubt,
And you never can tell how close you are,
It may be near when it seems so far,
So stick to the fight when you're hardest hit--
It's when things seem worst that you must not quit.

- Author Unknown

PUTTING IT ALL TOGETHER

So, what is the one thing more important than understanding all of the principles? **Understanding how they all work together!** Each principle may be equated to a muscle in your body. It may be great to have nice biceps but if the rest of your body is out of shape then it takes away from your great biceps. Your body is an organism that works together in harmony. Likewise, these principles are designed to work together for you to create prosperity for yourself and others. Regardless of whether you are religious or not even science is beginning to acknowledge the improbability that the universe and intelligent life could've evolved simply by chance. Suggesting that organized systems of galaxies, solar systems, planets and balanced ecological systems would have the ability to form themselves is equivalent to saying you can simply throw buckets of paint on the wall and end up with Michelangelo's Sistine Chapel ceiling as the result!

We are all, natural creators; it is simply a matter of learning to optimize our abilities to create any experience of our choosing. An Intelligent Force/Spirit/God creates and sustains the universe and we as individual souls have the ability to create on a smaller scale but in equal fashion. It matters not what you may "attract" in life; what matters is your ability to create anything you need to prosper and be happy under **any** circumstances. We literally bring ideas from an unmanifested state and through choice, will, vision, action, energy, resolve and reciprocity create technologies, institutions, pieces of art, music, political systems, businesses, corporations and anything imaginable from the subtlest state into gross form for the masses to utilize. Thus, we have the acronym for **P.R.O.S.P.E.R.I.T.Y.** to help you quickly recall the essential steps toward being in control of yourself, your life and your creations. So, let's break down this acronym and examine it in its parts:

"Principle Reasons...
Optimistic Service...
Produces Exponential Richness...
Inevitably...
Through You!"

Principle Reasons: These are the fundamental reasons or causes of how we create. Man is a unique being. There are three parts to every individual human being. We are spirit, mind and body. All things observable begin with spirit. Spirit is inherently being, consciousness and bliss. The fact that **you exist** is the essence of being. **Knowing** that you exist is consciousness. Bliss is the **natural state** of being and consciousness for it is complete unto itself. In truth, we need nothing outside of ourselves to be blissful. Our minds serve as the bridge between our spirit and the physical experience of our bodies. Most of us through improper understanding and learned bad behaviors forget that we are creators and instead develop weak minds that become slaves to what our experiences tell us. If you ever watch a child play, they allow the power of their imaginations to create fantastical worlds for their enjoyment. All a kid needs are a cardboard box and some company to have a world of fun. Throughout the experience of education and learning we only nurture one side of our brains, mostly the rational side, and fail to nurture our creative and artistic side. We must re-learn how to use our creative imaginations to experience anything we choose. Lastly, our bodies serve as vehicles for us to interact in this world of relativity. Two important facts to remember are that:

1. You are not your body. Your body is simply an instrument for you to experience all sorts of things.
2. All things of the physical world are temporary.

Our goals are to enjoy the things of this world but do not be attached to them. The essence of who you are far surpasses any attainment of life. Never be a slave to your desires, possessions or experiences. These principle reasons are tools or guidelines to help you navigate easily and smoothly in this world of duality. As you strengthen your ability to manipulate and utilize these principles then they will behave as "laws" for you, but it is important to remember that in the process of mastering these principles you must first change yourself. It is a mutual process. As you mold these principles, they equally mold you. As you become refined in your essence, you will ascend to a point where you will eventually be able to *speak* and *so it is*!

Optimistic Service: We cannot change the world; we can only change ourselves. Therefore, the best thing we can do in interaction with the world, people being the most important, is to serve others by fulfilling needs and leading by example. As we give unto others, life gives to us in equal or greater measure. As we give to others the best energy, we can serve them with is optimism and enthusiasm. The more unselfish, genuine and sincere we are, the greater positive forces for good we become, and we inspire others to do the same. Worry not if everyone you encounter doesn't respond positively to your service. Remember, your goal isn't to change people or to have expectations of return. Nothing you do goes in vain. The energy you put out will return to you no matter what. Every experience we have, whether favorable or not, is a learning opportunity. If you experience something that wasn't what you intended, always ask yourself, "What could I have done differently to create a different experience"? Mahatma Gandhi stated, ***"You must be the change you seek in the world!"***

Produces Exponential Richness: True richness isn't a measure of your bank account. It is a measure of your overall well-being. Being fulfilled and content in body, mind and spirit is your goal and a proper assessment of your prosperity. Every thought we entertain, every word we speak and every action we take creates an effect in the world and the people around us. This energy is multiplied depending upon how the "universe" receives it. If you put out positive, well-intended energy then that is multiplied and returned to you. Even if everyone doesn't receive your positive energy as you may have hoped for is not a reason to fret. Everyone is a "work in progress." Rather than focus on the bad, focus on the good and this shall be your relative experience. When you are able to maintain your peace of mind and inner bliss, then your experiences will have less of an impact on you. We are creators. Realize you never have to be a victim. If you don't like the experience... create another!

Inevitably: These principles are unfailing. Whether you believe in gravity or not you are subject to its pull. Whether you believe in Newton's Laws of Motion or Einstein's Law of Relativity or not doesn't change their impact. Your ability to use these "Laws of Nature" to your benefit will in time allow you to see the world with a clarity unlike ever before. When that time comes, your consciousness will transcend even these physical laws. The Matrix was a fictional story, but it was based upon ancient Zen philosophy, which embodies universal truths. When Neo evolved in his understanding of the nature of the "matrix" he was able to see the code behind all objects. He then became able to manipulate the dream world at his choosing. Likewise, the inevitable conclusion will come when one day your presence has been purified to the point where you will understand the world from a higher perspective and the things that control others will no longer be able to control you in the same way.

Through You: Things don't really happen to us. We don't truthfully attract things. All that we experience is ultimately the outward experience of what we created. They are the result of either our conscious or subconscious choosing. Accepting responsibility for all our "good" and "bad" experiences empower us to change or create another. As long as you accept that someone else created something for you, you lessen your ability to do anything about it. Never become fixated with things having to go your way. Establish your purpose. Strengthen your vision and **create** your experience.

I suggest your approach in incorporating these principles be smooth and controlled. I use the analogy of how, as children, we used to blow bubbles. Our bubbles represent our prosperity. In order to blow an actual bubble, you must properly soak your wand in the soapy bubble solution. As you blow into the wand, you must blow steadily. If you don't blow hard enough then no bubble forms. Likewise, if you blow too hard or fast then your bubble bursts immediately. Remember the story of the Golden Egg! In order to blow a large beautiful bubble, your hand must be steady and your breath smooth and controlled. As your bubble of prosperity expands, you should allow it to encompass everyone you care for indiscriminately without judgment. This way you carry all those you love with you and their contributions increase the overall lot for everyone. With great sincerity, your prosperity bubble can encircle the entire world with everyone in it. Let nothing deter you from your ultimate goals yet unselfishly include others. Inside you is infinite potential but you must be the catalyst through your own self-effort and free choice. All change must come from within…

EPILOGUE:
THE GOLDEN EGG

In yoga they tell us that the soul wears three bodies – the causal body, astral body and the physical body. Most of us are clearly aware of our physical body but not our astral or causal bodies. This book was written to take a subject matter near and dear to most of us, the well-being of our bodies and livelihoods, and lead us to something much greater and significant. The majority of people seek comfortable livings because it brings us pleasure and freedom in this world. However, regardless of your achievements and acquisitions in this world they are all temporary. Whether you obtain all the riches in the world or not, the time will come for you to depart this life. Therefore, this book was designed to use your desires for "worldly sweeteners" and guide you to the sweetest honey found within!

There are eight limbs in yoga: 1. Yamas (Universal Morality) 2. Niyamas (Personal Observances) 3. Asanas (Body Postures & Physical Conditioning) 4. Pranayama (Life Force Control) 5. Pratyahara (Control and Withdrawal of the Senses) 6. Dharana (Concentration) 7. Dhyana (Meditation) and 8. Samadhi (Spiritual Ecstasy). The principles in this book are designed to cause a shift in one's consciousness. To help you see yourself and your life's experiences from a new perspective. You will develop the ability to separate your awareness from ego and physical body identification.

The most important parts of this book are developing concentration and the ability to look within. Being still and "looking within" will in time lead one to Dhyana known as meditation. Meditation is a state of being. One cannot truly "meditate" because that is a verb and it suggests doing something. Meditation is stillness and being free from restlessness and activity.

As one progresses through the eight limbs of yoga, it leads to a transcendental state of being which will ultimately transform your entire life. Your experience of life will be forever changed because all the things you once sought externally outside yourself, you now realize are within. The Source of eternal prosperity is within you. As taught by Swami Satyananda Saraswati, as you go within and your concentration deepens you will gradually begin to feel your astral body and perceive your astral body as a point. Continue to concentrate on that point. That point becomes recognized as the form of a golden egg.

Make the determination to focus all of your awareness entirely on this golden egg. It will gradually begin to expand; almost spontaneously. Continue to watch it carefully. This golden egg appears to be luminous and glowing without emitting any rays of light. Continue to focus on it and the egg will become larger and larger. It will continue to take form and give off light. This golden egg is the dazzling form of your Karana Sharir or causal self. Yet expect nothing... and then... Dhyana (the meditative state of being) which leads to samadhi – Spiritual Bliss!

"What lies behind us... and what lies before us... are tiny matters compared to what lies within us!"
Ralph Waldo Emerson

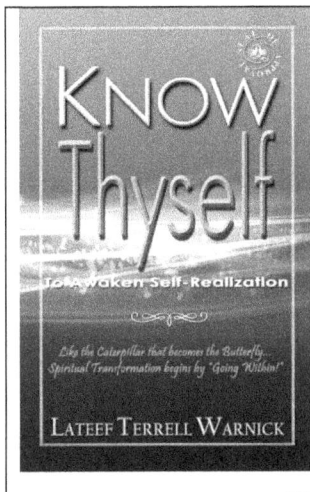

"Know Thyself – To Awaken Self-Realization"
(ISBN: 193919914X)
by **Lateef Terrell Warnick**

"WHO AM I?" is the most important question in life you'll ever ask yourself! Yet many will go to their graves without ever finding a concrete answer to this question. There is one purpose to life and that is to come to **"Know Thyself!"**

One's inner search brings the awareness and direct experience of Spirit. This is accomplished through three phases of Evolution, Experience and Enlightenment.

Evolution: The Book of Genesis symbolically represents how the world comes into being. The formless Spirit mystically descends, taking form, within creation.

Experience: Everything that we experience in this world of duality is what we call life. Through infinite possibilities, we make choices and are intended to grow and evolve but where are we going?

Enlightenment: Many take the Book of Revelation to mean "Armageddon" thus feeding fear of the end of the world. But what if hidden within these pages were secrets towards man's spiritual enlightenment?

Published by **1 S.O.U.L. Publishing**. Purchase at all major retailers like Amazon, Barnes & Noble & Books-a-Million for just $14.95 or directly at **www.onassiskrown.com** for just $12.95 plus shipping & handling.